# LAROCCA
## MAFIA CRIME FAMILY

*The Complete History of*
*A Pittsburgh Criminal Organization*

MAFIA LIBRARY

© **Copyright 2025 - All rights reserved.**

The content contained within this book may not be reproduced, duplicated or transmitted without direct written permission from the author or the publisher.

Under no circumstances will any blame or legal responsibility be held against the publisher, or author, for any damages, reparation, or monetary loss due to the information contained within this book, either directly or indirectly.

**Legal Notice:**

This book is copyright protected. It is only for personal use. You cannot amend, distribute, sell, use, quote or paraphrase any part, or the content within this book, without the consent of the author or publisher.

**Disclaimer Notice:**

Please note the information contained within this document is for educational and entertainment purposes only. All effort has been executed to present accurate, up to date, reliable, complete information. No warranties of any kind are declared or implied. Readers acknowledge that the author is not engaged in the rendering of legal, financial, medical or professional advice. The content within this book has been derived from various sources. Please consult a licensed professional before attempting any techniques outlined in this book.

By reading this document, the reader agrees that under no circumstances is the author responsible for any losses, direct or indirect, that are incurred as a result of the use of the information contained within this document, including, but not limited to, errors, omissions, or inaccuracies.

# TABLE OF CONTENTS

Introduction ..................................................................................... 1

**Chapter 1 : The First Dons Of Pittsburgh** ................................. 7
    The Banana King ........................................................................ 9
    The Neapolitan War ................................................................ 12
    American Prohibition .............................................................. 17

**Chapter 2 : The Booze Barons** .................................................. 23
    Calderone And The Roaring '20s ............................................ 24
    Blood And Steel ....................................................................... 27
    Poor Joe Siragusa .................................................................... 33

**Chapter 3 : The Plagues Of Wylie Avenue** ............................. 39
    Bazzano And The House Of Volpe ......................................... 39
    The Mafia Commission .......................................................... 46

**Chapter 4 : The Steel City Mafia** ............................................. 53
    Old Habits, New Don .............................................................. 54
    The Rise Of Big John Larocca ................................................ 60

**Chapter 5 : The Larocca Family** .............................................. 65
    The Road To Apalachin ........................................................... 65
    Cops, Casinos, And Communists ........................................... 74

**Chapter 6 : Damage Control** ............................................................. **81**
    Trouble In Paradise ................................................................... 81
    The "Other" Genovese ................................................................ 85

**Chapter 7 : New Turf, New Bosses** ................................................ **91**
    The Coup Of Rochester ............................................................. 91
    Lines Of Succession ................................................................... 96

**Chapter 8 : Genovese Ascendant** ................................................ **101**
    The Cleveland War .................................................................. 103
    The New Pittsburgh Regime .................................................. 106

**Chapter 9 : The Death Of The Steel City Mafia** ..................... **113**

**Conclusion** ......................................................................................... **119**

**References** ......................................................................................... **121**

# INTRODUCTION

The 36 floors of New York City's famous and luxurious Warwick Hotel stand tall on the corner of Manhattan's Sixth Avenue. The Warwick had a prestigious reputation, and their guestbook included some of the most world famous entertainers like Elvis Presley, The Beatles, and Dean Martin. The Warwick prided itself on being a popular venue to host business meetings and cocktail parties in their attached restaurant.

But, one afternoon in the summer of 1958, the Warwick was also host to a particular business deal that was not quite as "above board" as those of their other politician and show business guests. On this day, a man named Joseph Merola was meeting with Abe Seid, to whom he delivered $4,000 in cash (U.S. Government, 1961). Seid, better known by his pseudonym "Al Ross," was a Russian national with apparently strong connections to the Italian-American Mafia in the northeast. Merola clearly had plenty of crooked connections too, as the $4,000 that he handed to Seid was only a down payment for what turned out to be a large shipment of illegal firearms. Merola, who was actually a "made man" in the Pittsburgh Mafia, promised Seid the rest of the money, and Seid took him at his word because he was going to be very eager to offload these weapons. Merola didn't know it yet, but the guns and ammunition he just paid for in advance were the property of the United States military, and they were going to want them back.

Also unknown to Merola was the fact that his boss, a Pittsburgh bigshot mobster named Sam Mannarino, was fully aware of the deal at the Warwick and what was going on, and in fact, Seid's shipment of guns was actually destined for him. It's not clear whether Merola's superiors were manipulating him or whether they simply had the same plans, but shortly after his meeting with Seid, once Merola discovered that Mannarino was looking to acquire an airplane to use for the transportation of firearms, he knew that he was being fooled, or at worst, double-crossed.

When Merola later discovered that the weapons had belonged to the military, and had only recently been heisted from a National Guard armory depot in Canton, Ohio, he didn't want anything to do with the plan. Not that it mattered much, though, because if Sam Mannarino wanted those weapons, then he was getting them. Sam and his brother Gabriel were two of the kings of Pittsburgh, and as far south as Florida, the Mannarino name carried a lot of weight. There were only a few people that could tell them what to do, and Joe Merola wasn't one of them. Besides, where Seid had sourced the weapons was shocking enough, but it sounded like a petty misdemeanor compared to what the Pittsburgh Mafia planned to do with them.

Beginning in 1956, the island nation of Cuba, less than 100 miles off the coast of Florida, was engaged in a bloody civil war. Fidel Castro and his band of Cuban revolutionaries were fighting to oust the brutal dictator Fulgencio Batista, who just so happened to be one of America's closest allies in the Caribbean (U.S. Government, 1961;

Vallin, n.d.). The Italian-American Mafia has a long and complicated history with Cuba, which will be a subject dealt with in the following chapters, but what the Mannarinos and the Pittsburgh crime Family were plotting in 1958 was easily the most audacious play the Mafia had ever made on the island. The stolen cache of Carbine rifles, M-1 Garands, and other assorted weaponry and ammunition was destined for the Cuban rebels, who had made significant gains toward the capital city of Havana by 1958. The Pittsburgh Mafia planned on smuggling weapons stolen from the National Guard into Cuba in order to aid in the overthrow of an American foreign ally.

For an organized crime Family that was merely a fraction of the size of any one of the infamous Five Families of New York City, this was an incredibly brazen scheme. And, what was it all for? What could they possibly stand to gain from burglarizing the government and participating in a foreign civil war? The answer was simple: casino dollars. To safeguard the millions of dollars they skimmed from their gambling interests in Cuba, these gangsters were willing to do the unthinkable: to interfere in international politics. Just as surprising is the fact that this gun smuggling scheme went directly against the general Mafia's stance on the war in Cuba. Other national Mafia outfits, including the Five Families as well as the Midwest and Florida Families, actively supported Batista against Castro's rebels because of how amicable the Cuban government had been for years toward American gangsters and their business.

However, the Pittsburgh Family, which was headed by the illustrious John S. LaRocca, was more forward-looking: They correctly believed that Batista, their longtime ally, was a thing of the past, and that Fidel Castro would be the islands future. By delivering them a bounty of weapons to aid their struggle, the Pittsburgh gangsters hoped to get in on the ground floor of a truly prosperous relationship, and to win the favor of a potentially sympathetic Castro government.

This future-oriented approach defined and characterized the most successful decades of the Pittsburgh Mafia. But, how did they become so powerful in the first place? Even at their peak, the Pittsburgh Family had no more than a few dozen members, and only a handful of local captains or *capos* that ran operations at a local level. When compared to the powerful New York Families, the crew that John LaRocca led in the 1950s had quite humble beginnings, and only achieved regional dominance after decades of struggle.

Like in New York, the criminal environment in Pittsburgh was anything but hospitable. At the turn of the 20th century, the criminal underworld of western Pennsylvania was deeply fractured along ethnic lines. Irish gangs, Black gangs, and Jewish crime syndicates all participated in Pittsburgh's various criminal rackets and violently wrestled for more control. Over the long term, the Italian Mafia was certainly the most successful, but this was only achieved through years of bloodshed. Even within the various disorganized Italian gangs in early 1900s, Pittsburgh's territory was subdivided by regional ethnicity. The Sicilians in the north and south sides of the city that belonged to the Mafia tended not to collaborate with their Calabrian counterparts, who had their own separate 'Ndrangheta organization. The east side Neapolitans, too, claimed their own territory for the feared Camorra, the organization that once was more powerful than even the Mafia.

By 1958, when the audacious Cuban weapons fiasco took place, the other ethnic segments of the Italian-American underworld had either been utterly destroyed by or forcefully amalgamated into the Mafia long ago. The structure of the Mafia, which was birthed in Sicily, a small island off the coast of Southern Italy, quickly became the most dominant form of Italian organized crime all across both the United States and Southern Canada, and has since firmly entrenched itself in American popular culture. Classic pieces of cinema like *The Godfather, Goodfellas,* and *Casino* are all based on society's fascination with the Mafia and its secretive, brutalist nature.

The infamous Five Families deservedly claim the majority of attention both in print and on the big screen, but the Pittsburgh Family, led by the likes of John Bazzano, "Big John" LaRocca, Michael Genovese, and others, managed to become arguably one of the most powerful and regionally influential criminal syndicates in the nation. As we'll see, the tiny Pittsburgh clan even had the power to confront some of the most historically powerful Families, and actually managed to expand while their counterparts in New York, Buffalo, Philadelphia and elsewhere were crumbling under government onslaught.

The following chapters will tell the story of how a small, ethnically segregated clique of criminals became powerful enough to stage an international arms deal and influence foreign diplomacy. In many ways, the Pittsburgh Family was exceptional, but ultimately their fate was the same as every other Mafia outfit in the nation, and just like the Cuba scheme, it led only to utter disaster.

# CHAPTER 1
## THE FIRST DONS OF PITTSBURGH

In the late 1890s and early 1900s, the national Mafia was not only fractured and disorganized, it was also a relatively unknown entity. This was especially true in Pittsburgh, whose Sicilian population was not nearly as prominent as in New York City or Boston. Several generations of missteps and misfortunes eventually exposed the Mafia's existence to the government and society at large, but in these early years, mafiosi operated in almost complete obscurity. Many people had a general understanding that *some* kind of Italian criminal organization existed, and the police were certainly aware of it too, but few understood how it worked, who was in charge, or how deeply connected different Families were.

Police first began taking notice of threatening letters that made their way around Sicilian immigrant neighborhoods that carried threatening messages for local shop owners and businesses. They demanded perpetual cash tribute, and promised swift retribution if the demand wasn't met. The letters were often signed with a menacing symbol, like a skull or a hand print in ink. The police started referring to the mysterious organizations simply as "the Black Hand," (Cascio, 2021).

Much of this secrecy has to do with old Sicilian Mafia tradition. Like all newcomers, Italian immigrants brought with them many of their cultural practices, and out of the over one million Sicilian immigrants that arrived in the first decades of the 20th century, at least some were bound to have had Mafia connections in the old world. This was especially true when Italian dictator Benito Mussolini came to power in 1922 and began a brutal campaign in Sicily against the Mafia, who had almost free reign over the island prior to then (Ove, 2000). Mafiosi fled en masse to the United States, joining their brothers and cousins and uncles who had already brought the Mafia structure to America.

One of the most fundamental aspects of this structure is the core Mafia tenet of *omerta*, which is essentially a code of silence. Initiation into the Mafia required taking a vow to never divulge the existence of the Mafia to anyone outside of the Family, even their closest associates. If you got arrested for a crime, then you were expected to keep your mouth shut, even under the pain of death. You couldn't name accomplices or reveal the identity of anyone who may have ordered you to carry out the crime. To break *omerta* was a high crime, and although future generations faltered, the code of silence did much to conceal the earliest history of the Mafia.

Even for Salvatore Catanzaro, the first "known" boss of the Pittsburgh Mafia, most of what we have to go off of are rumors and suspicions. His multiple stabbings were certainly no coincidence, and he had several suspected "Black Hand" associates, but little hard evidence or testimony exists for Catanzaro's control over Sicilian crime in the city. What is known is that the tenure of Catanzaro marked the beginning of the Pittsburgh police's long, hard look into the so-called Black Hand.

## **The Banana King**

Salvatore Catanzaro was born in Sicily, most likely around Palermo in the 1850s. It isn't certain whether he was connected to the Mafia in Sicily, but it's likely that his family was somehow connected to the Palermo underworld. Sometime around 1879, Salvatore made his way to the United States in one of the earliest waves of Sicilian migration, accompanied by some of his family. After landing in New York City, he made his way to San Francisco, where he settled with his brother for some time.

There, on the West Coast, Salvatore and his brother most likely began their fruit and produce wholesale company, a precursor to the larger company they would control in Pittsburgh. After about five years in California, Salvatore returned briefly to his native Sicily to find a wife. He married, and soon after, sailed to America once again. From New York, Salvatore and his bride this time made their way to Western Pennsylvania, placing firm roots and starting a family in Pittsburgh. In 1888, the S. Catanzaro & Sons produce company was officially inaugurated, and Salvatore quickly made his way to the top of that business realm, earning the nickname "The Banana King," (Cascio, 2021).

With a name like that, there's no doubt that Catanzaro was successful. In reality though, the profits of the family business were always inflated because it was almost certainly used as a "front" for Catanzaro's illegal businesses (i.e., illicit profit was "laundered" through the fruit business as legitimate profit). While peddling bananas and oranges sounds like a harmless enough way to make a living, the produce business in this era was notoriously brutal and cutthroat. Distribution companies and wholesalers were surprisingly often run by gangsters who had ties back home and could secure oranges, lemons, eggplant, tomatoes, nuts, etc., for cheap and resell them in America.

Plus, considering the product they moved was fragile and prone to rotting, and preservation technology was still crude, ensuring their prompt delivery and unhindered passage was literally a matter of life and death. Even brief work stoppages could mean the loss of thousands of dollars (which was not chump change in the 1890s), and were often used against rival fruit merchants. If the trucks were to inexplicably catch fire for some reason, entire shipments would spoil. Labor disputes and hijackings were also common. It was in this vicious environment that Catanzaro established a name for himself, and he certainly did not earn the moniker "Banana King" by being a nice guy.

By 1900, Catanzaro had established himself as a well-respected local businessman in Pittsburgh's Italian community. Given his stature in the community, the Banana King was in a position to extort tribute money from other local Italian shop owners—a cultural practice that he imported from Sicily, along with his fruit. Tributes were collected via his loyal subordinates, who at the time most typically consisted of his close or extended family members, which was common among most early era Mafia Families.

Aside from extortion and moving oranges, Catanzaro, like every other Mafia boss, was almost certainly involved in all manner of organized crime. At the time, this included prostitution, gambling, numbers (also known as the Italian lottery), heists, loansharking, and more. Smuggling was also a Mafia mainstay, but Catanzaro never lived to see the glorious golden age of American Prohibition. Despite his racketeering, he had the veneer of an honest and upstanding citizen—his businesses across Western Pennsylvania appeared "clean," and he even served as the Treasurer for the Italian Red Cross chapter in Pittsburgh. Needless to say, his connections ran deep both in the legitimate world and the criminal one.

Unfortunately, his connections couldn't always save him from the enemies he had made in the crooked fruit trade. He was apparently very nearly stabbed to death in 1892 by an unknown assailant, and then survived another stabbing later in 1914. The last attack prompted Catanzaro to retire fully from organized crime, but he didn't have much time left to enjoy being out of the game. By 1916, he was dead, and the Pittsburgh Mafia—still a minor player in the grand scheme of things—was moving on from possibly its earliest "Godfather," (Cascio, 2021).

At the time Catanzaro died, he was still operating S. Catanzaro & Sons Co., at least on paper. As far as the Pittsburgh police were concerned, he also died as nothing more than a good citizen. To the old school mafiosi, even his enemies, the old traditions still meant something in this time, and none divulged Catanzaro's criminal dealings. For decades to come, both local and federal law enforcement would drive themselves crazy trying to prove the existence of some kind of organized Sicilian syndicate.

## **The Neapolitan War**

When Catanzaro retired in 1914, the next man to take the top spot in Pittsburgh's Sicilian quarters was Gregorio Conti. While Catanzaro's past is shaky, and we have to rely on inferences to establish his criminality, Gregorio Conti was a hardened mafioso through and through. Some even consider Conti to be the first "true" boss of Pittsburgh, because his reign began the first steps toward consolidating the wider Italian underworld (The American Mafia, n.d.). When Conti stepped into the boss role, Pittsburgh was still deeply ethnically divided; certain territories were off limits for the Calabrians, Sicilians, Neapolitans, and so on. Ethnic tension between gangs was a concern under Catanzaro, but under Conti, these troubles were brought to a boil.

Gregorio Conti was a few years younger than his predecessor, having been born in March 1873 (sources vary, some claim 1874) in the central Sicilian town of Comitini to parents Gesua and Giacomo. At the time, Comitini was a major sulfur mining town, which meant that the Sicilian Mafia likely also had a significant presence in the area. The crews that worked the sulfur mines are believed by some to have been the first to adopt what we know as the Mafia code and way of life, and in the sulfur pits is possibly where the Mafia structure first took shape (The American Mafia, n.d.). Although any early Mafia connections Conti may have had in Comitini can't be confirmed, it is also known that he operated a wine and spirits business before he migrated to America. The local liquor industry was another typical Mafia racket, and Conti brought his expertise in the business with him when he left Sicily for the United States.

In September 1907, Conti departed from the port of Palermo, destined for New York City. In tow with him were his nephew, Giuseppe Cusumano, as well as Vincenzo Terrana. Their intention was to travel to Pittsburgh to link up with Gregorio's older brother, Gaetano Conti, who had settled in the city some years earlier. Gaetano had already made quite a name for himself in Pittsburgh's Hill District by running a respectable medical practice as a physician. The three men in Gregorio's party also appear to have been at least somewhat educated—Cusumano was apparently a trained chemist, and Terrana was a surgeon.

Unfortunately, the men had other avenues of earning a living in mind. Crime appears to have been a constant for the Conti family, at least for as long as they had been in America. In 1909, Gaetano was implicated in a government fraud scheme where he would provide falsified medical documents for Italian immigrants who were looking to avoid being called for military service in their native Italy (The American Mafia, n.d.). At the time, Gaetano held the office of the official physician for the Italian consulate in Western Pennsylvania, so when the news broke that he was crooked, it was a major blow to his reputation. Undeterred, Gregorio and his companions continued to work with Gaetano, who was also involved with the Pittsburgh Mafia. Not long after this, it is believed that Gregorio Conti became the protégé of Salvatore Catanzaro.

By 1913, Gregorio became a naturalized American citizen, and soon after that, he was able to bring his wife and children over from Sicily to join him after six long years. Around the same time, Conti re-entered the alcohol business and opened Pittsburgh Wine & Liquors on Wylie Avenue in Hill District, just down the street from

Gaetano's medical office. His nephew, Giuseppe "Peppino" Cusumano, worked closely with Gregorio in the wine trade. Legal liquor provided good income for the Contis, but they quickly looked for alliances in other industries to expand into. Unlike Sal Catanzaro and the majority of other Sicilians at the time, Conti was more than willing to work with other ethnic factions, including Calabrians, the Neapolitan Camorra, African-Americans, and Jews—for now, at least. Just a few years into Conti's reign, he had made strong connections all across Pittsburgh and Western Pennsylvania, while he maintained complete control of Hill District, his home base.

Sometime around 1915, the Contis linked up with a mobster named Nicola "Nick" Gentile, which amplified the Pittsburgh Mafia's underworld ties. Gentile got his start working with the Kansas City Mafia, and had developed a relationship with powerful NYC gangsters like Charles "Lucky" Luciano, Vito Genovese, and Vincent Mangano by the time he went to Pittsburgh. He was certainly an up-and-comer, and Gentile would later serve as a respected mob "elder statesman," but when he first joined with Conti, he was mostly concerned with eliminating his competition and establishing both a name for himself and a base of power under Conti's leadership.

For the first couple years of Conti's reign, he and Gentile allowed and participated in a scheme run by the Neapolitans to extort Sicilians in Mafia-controlled neighborhoods, even within Hill District, something that likely never would have been tolerated under Catanzaro, or even Conti's successors. But, Conti gave the nod because his alliances with the Camorra were profitable. Besides, allowing them to operate in their territory was only means to an end—within months, Conti and his new capo Gentile were crafting plans to eliminate the Neapolitans completely.

At the time, the Camorra was the largest single Italian criminal organization (The American Mafia, n.d.). Mafiosi technically outnumbered the Neapolitans, but they were spread out across several crews that did not always cooperate. It was going to be a difficult task, but Conti was undeterred. By the end of 1916, the Hill District Mafia, headed by the Contis, Gentile, and their associates, was waging a bloody war against their Italian rivals. The Calabrians were the weakest ethnic group in the city, but the Camorra, headed by the Neapolitans Ferdinand Mauro and his top capo and enforcer Fortunato Calabro, suffered most significantly.

The first few months of the Neapolitan War saw many Mafia deaths, and many more properties burned or firebombed. Before long though, Conti had turned the tables on Mauro and his Neapolitan comrades. By the end of 1917, the Hill District Mafia had pushed well past their boundaries, and had conquered much Camorra territory. By the end of the year, the Neapolitan faction, as well as the Calabrian one, were almost completely destroyed (The American Mafia, n.d.). Their leadership was either dead or, if they were lucky, were on the lam and unofficially retired from organized crime.

The Sicilian faction had asserted dominance, and the Pittsburgh Mafia was on the rise. What little remained of the city's Neapolitan faction was eventually amalgamated into the Mafia as soldiers and associates enlisted with Conti's crews. However, it's unknown whether any of these Neapolitans or Calabrians were "made" (i.e., officially inducted) into the Mafia, as most Sicilian bosses in these early years demanded that members be 100% Sicilian on both their mother and father's side. Conti proved to be relatively progressive compared to most bosses of the era, so induction of these men was possible, especially considering that the New York Mafia did not yet control the membership of other Families in the country.

Regardless of whether the Sicilians' rivals were ever officially in the Mafia, their ranks were swelled by the income of new associates and collaborators. Black and Jewish gangs still posed a threat to the Mafia, and their territory was still off-limits, but Conti no longer had any real competition in the city from his fellow Italians, and Conti's reign saw the first true iteration of a united Pittsburgh Italian Mafia that was more than just an ethnic Sicilian enclave. As we'll see, future bosses took a different perspective on cooperation with non-Sicilians, but for now, at least, there was peace. Gregorio Conti and Nicola Gentile were now both very powerful men, but new challenges would soon arise for the new dons of Pittsburgh.

In 1918, Nick Gentile and his partners, Sam DiBella and Orazio Leone, were all indicted and tried for conspiring to defraud grocery suppliers. Gentile and Conti both owned grocery marts and their Mafia underlings helped to run them, but Conti was accused of stiffing the suppliers for tens of thousands of dollars worth of product. In Spring of that year, all three gangsters were convicted. The men decided to appeal the decision, and Conti was scrambling to do anything he could to get his men free. As a personal favor to Gentile, the don arranged for fellow fruit merchant and old-school Sicilian J.C. Catalano to personally put up $4,000 to bail Gentile out of prison while he appealed his court ruling (The American Mafia, n.d.).

At some point though, Gentile must have gotten wise and realized the appeal was doomed. Rather than stick around for his inevitable prison time, he decided to skip out on his bail and flee to his native Sicily until the heat died down. This caused some immediate problems for Conti, whom Catalano now held responsible for Gentile's debts. Rather than spark a new underground war, Conti decided just to settle up with Catalano and pay Gentile's debt.

## **American Prohibition**

For the remainder of 1918, things progressed relatively smoothly for Conti, especially considering he had just lost Gentile—the connected gangster who had quickly become one of the top advisors and enforcers for the Pittsburgh Family. The heat between the don and J.C. Catalano was also quieting down. Or, at least that is what Conti believed. As we'll see, it appears there may have been some bad blood between the two Sicilian businessmen that lingered too long. For now though, there were far more immediate problems at hand.

In 1918, as the First World War in Europe was winding to a close, the American government passed the Wartime Prohibition Act, restricting the sale and manufacture of substances containing more than 1.2% alcohol (Kenny, Burns, & McGill, 2022). The Act was supposedly designed to preserve grain rations for the war effort, but in reality, the American temperance movement had been looking for an excuse to lobby the government into banning alcohol for years. It was a great win for the temperance movement, but a significant problem for Gregorio Conti. Conti's main legitimate business was, of course, his Pittsburgh Wine & Liquor business, and with the Wartime Prohibition Act banning the sale of all hard liquor, wines, and the majority of beer, he was soon to be shut down by the government. One source of hope for Conti was that the Act was only meant to be temporary and was supposed to be repealed after the First World War ended. Funny enough, the Act didn't actually come into full effect until the war in Europe was already over.

Unfortunately, the evangelicals in American Congress were in no big rush to allow liquor to flood the streets again, and it was not long before the government passed the Volstead Act, officially banning liquor for consumption indefinitely. Unlike the Wartime Act, this new Congressional law would define American society and culture for over a decade. At the beginning of 1920, the law came into effect, and Conti's main source of legitimate income had now become a federal crime. America was now a dry country. For the up-and-coming generation of mobsters, Prohibition would prove to be an incredibly lucrative period, and many believe that the opportunities provided by manufacturing and selling illegal alcohol is what first propelled the Mafia into national power and prevalence. But for Conti, an aging gangster who was now without any real way to launder his illicit income, it was debatable whether he would be agile enough to adapt to the new way of life in the underworld. In short order, he was forced to shut down Pittsburgh Wine & Liquors and sell off as much of his stock as he could. The sun was setting on Gregorio Conti's reign.

Rather than try to break into the nascent bootlegging and smuggling market that was birthed with the advent of American Prohibition, Conti chose to simply take his fortunes and move back to Sicily with his family, abandoning his American businesses altogether. Unfortunately, it seems the old Pittsburgh don's greed got the better of him. He apparently wanted to make one last big score before he fled the United States, and he was still in possession of a sizeable inventory of alcohol that the government now decided was illegal. Conti arranged a deal to get rid of the last of his stock, but he reportedly mislabeled all the bottles and charged several times more than what they were actually worth. If that wasn't bad enough, he was also suspected of scamming other young bootleggers into buying over 100 cases of bottles labeled as whisky, which were instead filled with water from a nearby river on Conti's order. Needless to say, in his last few weeks in the United States, Conti had made himself quite a few new enemies.

However, as far as Conti was concerned, he was already in the clear. He was a respected man with a lot of money and influence, and soon enough, he would be halfway across the world. He had already secured passports for himself and his family and they were scheduled to depart in September of 1919, just months after the Volstead Act passed in Congress. Still, Conti knew he couldn't linger too long. The passports he secured were expedited under the false pretense that Conti's wife had urgent and dire family matters to attend to in Sicily. They planned to take a train from Pittsburgh to New York City, and from there, they would sail across the Atlantic, eventually arriving in Sicily sometime in October. Unfortunately, the night before Gregorio Conti was scheduled to leave Pittsburgh with his wife, the don was shot four times through the back as he sat waiting in his car outside the Polish Catholic Church in Pittsburgh's Allegheny Valley (*Man slain in shadow of church* (1919, September 24), The Pittsburgh Press).

On September 24, the Pittsburgh Press reported the death of Conti, aged 45, and claimed that witnesses saw three men fleeing on foot from the scene after the shots were heard. As it turned out, Conti had been in the car along with J.C. Catalano, his relative Philip Catalano, as well as Orazio Leone (the same man who had been convicted of fraud along with Gentile back in 1918). The paper outright accused these three men of orchestrating the shooting, and Pittsburgh Police Commissioner Charles Johnston claimed that it was some kind of "blackhand plot" (*Man slain in shadow of church* (1919, September 24), The Pittsburgh Press). One witness told police that they saw the man seated behind the driver lean forward and press an object against the back of the driver's seat right before hearing two loud pops. By the time police arrived, Conti was the only one left in the vehicle, and the don's body was found with two passports for himself and his wife in his pocket, covered in blood. He was quickly taken to St. Francis hospital, but was declared dead upon arrival. Once again, no hard evidence existed for Mafia involvement in the crime, and no mention was made in the paper about Conti heading up the Pittsburgh Mafia.

The three men spotted fleeing the scene were identified and later arrested, but all three of them claimed that Conti was a dear friend of theirs. According to them, the actual murderer was some unknown figure that they saw approach from the side of the car and shoot through the window into the back seat, killing their friend and sending them into a panic. The chief detective, Officer Clyde

Edeburn, openly doubted that it could have been possible for anyone outside the car to have murdered Conti, but it didn't matter.

Amazingly, all three men were released, and no murder charges were filed against them. It appears overwhelmingly likely, however, that Catalano had unfinished business with Conti. It's possible that Catalano never forgave Conti for talking him into bailing Gentile out of jail. Or, perhaps Conti made the wrong people upset with his bottled river water scam, and Catalano either got ripped off or was paid by those who did get ripped off to take care of Conti. Regardless, the bottom line was that the don of the Pittsburgh Mafia was now dead, and no one was ever charged with his murder.

The beginning of the Prohibition era was marked with a dramatic tragedy for the Western Pennsylvania underworld, but the incoming power-sharing council of leaders that took hold of the city after Conti's death was gearing up to profit massively off the new status quo. The following decade would be one of unimaginable success, and of endless bloodshed.

# CHAPTER 2
## THE BOOZE BARONS

The dawn of Prohibition in America is what allowed the Pittsburgh Mafia to truly come into its own. Since the late 19th century, Mafia Families (as well as the Camorra and 'Ndrangheta, for that matter) relied almost completely on what we would call small-time crimes. Shopkeepers were extorted for "protection" money, prostitutes were pimped out in their brothels, and illegal card games were held in the backrooms of local shops. Sometimes a bank would get robbed, or a jewelry store would be heisted, and there were always predatory loansharking operations, but everyone always preferred to keep violence to a minimum unless it was absolutely necessary. The money they were earning just wasn't worth arousing the attention of law enforcement.

However, with the introduction of Prohibition and the new bootlegging industry came profits like no one in the Pittsburgh underworld had ever seen before. It took a complete ban for everyone in America to realize just how much they loved getting drunk, and as long as there was someone willing to supply the booze, then breaking the law to get it was hardly a deterrent. Now, it seemed like every wise guy in the state wanted to get in on the action. In the underworld, competition led to violence. Unlike their illegal blackjack tables or back-alley whorehouses, this was income that the Pittsburgh Family was willing to die for.

## Calderone and the Roaring '20s

After Conti was gunned down, spoiling his retirement, there was a large void that needed to be filled in the Pittsburgh Mafia. His nephew, Peppino Cusumano, had been getting groomed by Conti for months to take reigns of the Family after he decided he was going to be fleeing to Sicily, but his murder prevented a peaceful transfer of power. Without that, Cusumano's inheritance was in question. Cusumano certainly had some support, mostly from those who were still loyal to his uncle, but young Cusumano simply didn't have the influence that Conti had, and maintaining complete control of Hill District, let alone the entire city, would have been a difficult task.

Despite the sway that Cusumano still held, he was not the only one calling the shots. A Mafia elder statesman named Salvatore Calderone was almost certainly involved in a power-sharing situation with Cusumano. At the time, Mafia activities in Western Pennsylvania were being overseen by a kind of unofficial panel of trusted senior mafiosi—similar to the New York City Mafia Commission, which had not yet been formed. Calderone was one of the key "chairmen" of this panel.

Salvatore Calderone was born in Sicily around 1858 and migrated to the United States sometime in the late 1890s, eventually moving to Pennsylvania and settling in Apollo, a small city about a 45-minute drive northeast from Pittsburgh. By the time Conti rose to power, Calderone was already a highly respected made guy in their side of Pennsylvania, and he had connections all over the Midwest, New York, and some regions in Canada. Although he never officially held the title of boss, many regard Calderone as the "man behind the curtain" and the real power behind Cusumano. Together, these two helped create a solid foundation for Mafia-controlled bootlegging in Pittsburgh and the surrounding area and they were able to take a firm hold of the illegal market.

They profited massively during the early years of Prohibition, which was a relatively peaceful period compared to the second half of the 1920s. Calderone ran a large bottling operation out of Apollo, which Cusumano took part in. Just like their predecessors, Calderone used his fruit and produce wholesale company to launder his illegal income and maintain the facade of an upstanding local businessman. In reality, they were running liquor, as well as supplying mass amounts of materials and ingredients to other bootleggers, including molasses, sugar, yeast, and grains. If you were a moonshiner in Western Pennsylvania in the early 1920s, the chances are that your supplies came from Calderone or Cusumano.

Across the nation, both federal, state, and local law enforcement actually had very little interest in enforcing the Prohibition laws. Many in the public saw bootlegging as a victimless crime and a harmless vice, and it was certainly better than losing your life savings at the roulette table or blowing all your cash on women. Besides that, most police officers enjoyed getting drunk as much as the next guy, so if they went and busted up their local moonshiners, they would be cutting off their own supply too.

Plus, the bootleggers weren't the only ones who could turn a profit in the business. The whole thing turned out to be incredibly lucrative for the cops as well. In many parts of the country in this era, police officers were woefully underpaid, which resulted in an eagerness to accept bribes in return for looking the other way when the bootleggers needed them to. The booze barons were making so much money that paying off a bunch of cops was a trivial matter, and it was certainly cheaper than losing an entire batch of whiskey to a police raid. The Bureau of Prohibition, which was a federal apparatus designed specifically to enforce the Volstead Act across the nation, was notoriously bloated, overly bureaucratic, and corrupt. Most of their agents were content to collect their paycheck while showing absolutely nothing in return for their money.

Given how much money there was to be made, and how much liquor Americans were eager to consume, it's no surprise that these early years went so smoothly for the Cusumano-Calderone alliance. With no real law enforcement attention to speak of, it seemed the good times would go on forever. Between 1919 and 1924, the whiskey-soaked underworld of Pittsburgh and Western Pennsylvania saw relatively few murders, as well as a high degree of cooperation between rival factions as well as the police and government agencies.

However, by 1925, this all changed. As the Pittsburgh Mafia approached the middle of the decade, Calderone began taking more and more of a backseat in running the Family. He was getting older, and if one thing was certain, it's that being a bootlegging kingpin was a young man's game. Sometime in 1925, the Mafia veteran retired altogether from day-to-day operations, and began serving instead as a trusted advisor to a range of bosses across the Midwest, including Kansas City and Chicago. Without the support and explicit endorsement of Calderone, Peppino Cusumano would have his work cut out for him. He knew there would be challengers, and it was unlikely that he would have the strength to stave them off. Indeed, by the end of 1925, Gregorio Conti's nephew was forced onto the sidelines, and a man named Stefano Monastero stepped in to take control of the Pittsburgh Mafia's bootlegging and smuggling operation (The American Mafia, n.d.; Lee, 2016).

## **Blood and Steel**

In the recent history of America, few cities were as important as Pittsburgh. Situated between the main Allegheny and Monongahela Rivers, Pittsburgh is where modern American industry was built. Rich supply of nearby coal, iron, and lumber made the city ideal for steel production, and the two large rivers provided easy transportation routes to deliver their steel across the nation. Prosperous factories, steel foundries and mills, and aluminum fabrication plants sprouted up all over the city, attracting millions looking for work in the new industrial powerhouse of the nation. By the 1920s, Pittsburgh was arguably the largest and most important industrial hub in the entire country, and the steel and metal produced there literally allowed America to revolutionize industries, build skyscrapers, and maintain infrastructure. Pittsburgh was forever after known as the "Steel City," but in the second half of the 1920s, the city was becoming famous for something else too: gangland-style shooting sprees and public executions (Mellon, n.d.). For the first time, blood was as abundant as steel, and much, much cheaper.

Stefano Monastero was born on March 3, 1889, in Caccamo, a small commune town within the major Sicilian port of Palermo. While still an infant, Stefano and his family migrated for the first time in 1889 or 1890, settling for a while in New Orleans, Louisiana. Stefano's father, Pietro Monastero, was a known mafioso back in Caccamo. Like most migrant mobsters, he apparently continued his criminal activity in his new home in America. In 1890, the police chief of New Orleans, David Hennessy, was publicly assassinated (The American Mafia, n.d.).

The "Black Hand" was suspected of being behind the execution, and the elder Monastero was charged and tried for allegedly orchestrating the hit, along with two of his associates. Pietro was never convicted of the crime, but it appears the locals were already convinced of his guilt. Shortly after the trial concluded, a mob of angry residents attacked Pietro and lynched him, along with the other two defendants in the case. Young Stefano's father avoided serving his prison sentence, but he couldn't avoid mob justice, exposing the future Pittsburgh mobster to extreme violence from a very young age. Violence turned out to be an almost constant factor in his life (The American Mafia, n.d.).

Sometime between 1905 and 1911, Stefano and his brothers (one of which was Sam, a future Mafia associate of Stefano) relocated once more to Western Pennsylvania. Stefano was still young at the time, and Pittsburgh is likely where he began following in his father's footsteps, getting involved with the local mobsters. His and his brothers' criminal careers likely started with petty crimes, but Stefano must have been involved in organized crime from an early age because he rose very quickly through the ranks of the Family under the reigns of Salvatore Catanzaro and Gregorio Conti.

By the time the Cusumano-Calderone diarchy came to power, Stefano had acquired a significant following of loyalists. When Prohibition hit, he was primed to start raking in cash. He grew his base of power, and by the time Calderone retired, he was prepared to seize control from Cusumano. It's not at all clear exactly how this transfer of power went down, and it's entirely possible that Cusumano peacefully retired in the face of obviously overwhelming competition. The Monasteros were powerful, and Stefano alone was enough to challenge Gregorio Conti's nephew. Rather than risk an underground war, which would have disrupted everybody's cash flow, it's likely that Cusumano just stepped down.

Once in power, it was Monastero's task to guide the Pittsburgh Mafia through the ultraviolent era of late-stage Prohibition. From 1925 onwards, the city's underworld changed drastically, and Monastero defined that change. Like his predecessors, Monastero provided the majority of bootleggers in the area with their supplies, particularly sugar, which he specialized in. An underling of Monastero, Giuseppe Siragusa became known in this period as the "Yeast Baron," because he was the primary supplier of the fermenting product to bootleggers all across Western Pennsylvania (Mellon, n.d.). He and Monastero also owned and operated several speakeasies in the city and around the state.

Monastero also massively swelled the Family ranks, recruiting many new associates and opening the books for a slew of new "made" guys. However, Monastero supposedly firmly believed in the value of blood relation, and preferred to induct relatives of already made guys. He focused particularly on immigrants from his own hometown of Caccamo the Palermo area. The desire for shared heritage restricted membership for other Sicilians, but despite this, the Pittsburgh Mafia reached their greatest size yet under Monastero.

Along with growing membership and profits came greater danger. Pittsburgh was no longer the peaceful paradise for bootleggers that it was under Calderone—competition from outside kicked in, and things were getting bloody. A few states over, in Chicago, Illinois, extreme violence had already been a daily occurrence for a few years by 1925. When Alfonse Capone, the most famous bootlegger and smuggler in history came to power, the streets of Chicago became even more dangerous. Not even police officers and federal agents were off-limits to Chicago gangsters if they threatened their bootlegging profits. The Chicago Outfit, which was co-founded and led by Capone, was a ruthless and brutal Mafia Family that snuffed out competition wherever and whenever they found it. This was in stark contrast to Pittsburgh, where cooperation, collusion, and peaceful bribery were king. Unfortunately, Chicago's brand of extreme violence was on its way to Pittsburgh, and appropriately enough, it was a Chicago gangster that brought it.

After countless Chicago gangsters got rich under Capone's regime, many tried to strike out on their own to build their own empires and rule their own territory. Others had been exiled from Chicago under threat of death because Al "Scarface" Capone had turned on them for one reason or another. It's not certain which of these best fits the profile of Luigi Lamendola, but this Chicago gangster brought plenty of trouble regardless.

Originally part of "The Outfit," Lamendola left Chicago in late 1925 and arrived in Pittsburgh, looking to claim the Steel City as his own

(Mellon, n.d.). To be a gangster in Chicago in 1925 meant that you had to be brazen, and you had to have a big ego. Lamendola put that on display when he swept into town and opened up his own speakeasy on Pittsburgh's Chatham Street in Hill District, which was the beating heart of the Pittsburgh Mafia's territory. The Capone outcast was clearly looking to ruffle feathers, but given the cooperative and relatively peaceful state of Pennsylvania's underworld, things with Lamendola should have gone smoothly for Monastero and his Family.

However, Lamendola was a product of the far more violent atmosphere. All he knew was an iron fist and aggressive domination. Soon after he rode into town and set up on Chatham Street, Lamendola issued a kind of edict to all the owners of local speakeasies and backroom pubs: They were to purchase their beer and whiskey from him, and him alone. Anyone who continued to buy from Monastero or the Pittsburgh capos were faced with threats, beatings, torchings, and even murder. Lamendola's arrival and his immediate play for power was a startling sign of things to come: Chicago-style violence was coming to Pittsburgh.

From this point on, being a bootlegger in the Steel City was a life-or-death business, and the faint of heart were easily exposed and weeded out. Monastero, however, proved to be more than up for the task, and was able to weather much of the violence that started erupting in 1926. Between then and 1933, there were more than 200 murders in Pittsburgh's Allegheny County alone (Mullen, 2021). More than a few of these could be attributed to Monastero.

Hill District, Homewood, and Larimer were the key battlegrounds for the ensuing bootlegger wars that the arrival of Lamendola sparked. The New Kensington and Wilkinsburg areas were particularly contentious. Monastero and Lamendola exchanged blows over the course of 1926, and the Pittsburgh Family leadership moved aggressively to snuff out the intruders from Chicago. Monastero's first real opportunity only came in 1927. One morning in May of that year, Lamendola was shot eight times directly in the face as he stepped out of the front door of his Chatham Street drunk house (Mellon, n.d.). And just like that, he was gone. Unfortunately, the gang wars, executions, and firebombings were here to stay. Everyone in Pittsburgh knew who was behind the brutal Lamendola murder, and both Stefano and his brother Sam were implicated in the investigation. They were questioned by police, but nothing ever came of it. Stefano Monastero walked out a victorious, free man.

Monastero continued to eliminate competition and anyone who threatened his liquor pipeline through 1927 and 1928. In 1929, the violence again came to a head when Stefano and Sam made moves to further secure his base of power. They orchestrated hits on several rival Hill District rum runners, and one of these men was named Joey "the Ghost" Pangallo. In September, Monastero's men carefully planted an explosive inside Pangallo's car and carefully wired it to explode upon ignition. The bomb did go off, and Pangallo was severely injured, but the hit failed to take his life (Ove, 2000).

This was actually the fourth time that Monastero allegedly tried and failed to take out Pangallo—once in 1927, an explosive went off directly under the driver's seat of his car and literally blew him through the roof into the air, and he *still* survived. Hilariously, Pangallo lasted several more years after Monastero's last attempt on his life, before finally dying of natural causes. Pangallo was far from Monastero's only target in Hill District—a local moonshiner named Morris Curran had his large office building completely destroyed by a bomb almost immediately after he set up shop in Pittsburgh Mafia territory—but the latest hit attempt on Pangallo was the last straw. Monastero had made an important enemy.

## Poor Joe Siragusa

On the road to the end of the decade, Monastero's rivals took shots at him too. His trucks were hijacked and his liquor stolen, and several of his men were killed, even in Hill District territory. The Pittsburgh Mafia was still the number one player in town by 1929, and there was no question as to who controlled the majority of the bootlegging market, but for Monastero personally, his latest failed hit on Joe Pangallo is what sealed his fate.

On August 6, 1929, Stefano and Sam Monastero took a trip to St. John's Hospital in Pittsburgh North Side to visit an associate of theirs (some sources say the associate was recovering from routine surgery, others claim he was the victim of a gangland shooting) (Mellon, n.d.; The American Mafia, n.d.). Unfortunately, the two brothers were followed there. The Monastero brothers knew that they had innumerable enemies in the city and that the two of them were targets, so Stefano always drove around in a custom bulletproof car. There was no chance of getting to him while he was inside, but almost immediately after the two brothers stepped out of the car to walk into the hospital, two unknown hitmen approached and unloaded clips onto each of them. Stefano was hit several times and collapsed onto the pavement, dying before medics arrived, thus ending yet another short reign for a Pittsburgh don.

Sam was hit as well, but survived his injuries. Stefano's brother eventually made a full recovery and attempted to continue to run his and his brother's businesses, but apparently the hatchet was not buried with Stefano's death, as Sam's body was found in March 1930, beaten and strangled to death with his own necktie in the driver's seat of his car. Immediately, Joe "the Ghost" Pangallo was suspected of orchestrating both Monastero murders. He was questioned by police and later was charged, but evidently was never convicted. This isn't at all surprising—around half of all gangland murders in the city between 1926 and the end of Prohibition in 1933 went unsolved (Lee, 2016).

The reign of Monastero, the man who established the Pittsburgh Family as the primary power in the Prohibition-era crime economy, was over. The next man to take the top spot was none other than the "Yeast Baron" Joe Siragusa. Siragusa had been in America since 1910, and had only moved to Pittsburgh years after that. When Prohibition hit, it took him barely any time to become the number one supplier of yeast to bootleggers in the western half of the state (Mellon, n.d.).

Befitting his moniker of "Baron," Siragusa lived with his large family in the upscale and ritzy Squirrel Hill neighborhood, on Beechwood Boulevard, fairly well isolated from the violence of the massive bootlegging supply empire that he ran. When Siragusa became boss of the Pittsburgh Family, there was still plenty of blood left to be shed in the era of Prohibition, which was approaching its 10th year in effect. For the time being, it was business as usual in the Steel City, but about 350 miles away in New York City, major developments were taking place that would affect every Mafia outfit in the nation.

Siragusa's reign is best defined by his relationship with the NYC Mafia Families, and by the birth of the "national Mafia." His reign also just happened to be when the NYC Mafia first began to really hold sway over mob politics in Pennsylvania. The Families there were growing significantly, and were eager to expand their power elsewhere over the smaller Families in Ohio, Michigan, Illinois, and Pennsylvania. Siragusa personally worked closely with the Castellammarese faction of the New York mob. At the time, this faction was headed by the illustrious Salvatore Maranzano, who soon became by far the number one gangster in the nation. In this period, Maranzano began "overseeing" Pittsburgh activity, and Joe Siragusa paid personal tribute to the New York boss (Mellon, n.d.; The American Mafia, n.d.; Mullen, 2021).

Having such a powerful interstate alliance was a significant boon for Siragusa in the first couple years of his leadership. Unfortunately, it also meant that Siragusa's fate was now tied to that of Maranzano, and Maranzano had plenty of enemies. Years prior to Siragusa's ascension, Sal Maranzano had been sent to New York City from his home in Sicily by the powerful Castellammare del Golfo Mafia Family. His mandate, as dictated by the legendary Don Vito Cascio Ferro, was to seize control of New York City's underworld on behalf of the Castellammarese Mafia. Maranzano, apparently one of Don Ferro's most trusted capos, almost certainly never intended to actually follow these orders. The Castellammare del Golfo flag was never going to be hoisted over New York, and he was never going to pay tribute to Don Ferro. He did, however, plan on taking over the city. When Don Ferro was sentenced to life in prison in 1930, this only reaffirmed Maranzano's independence. The faction that Maranzano built in New York was comprised almost entirely of fellow Castellammarese gangsters, and although Siragusa was not Castellammarese, the two bosses worked in tandem to secure his power.

In 1930, the same year that Maranzano's "boss" in Sicily was imprisoned, a massive power struggle known as the Castellammarese War broke out. The war was between the Castellammarese faction, headed by Maranzano, and the faction led by Joe "the Boss" Masseria, who prior to the war had been as the "boss of bosses." The outcome of this war would define Mafia politics for the next several generations, and although it's not clear exactly what role Siragusa had to play, he clearly made the wrong kind of enemies during the conflict. By April 1931, the war was over, and Maranzano and the Castellammarese clan were victorious. This was largely due to the support several Masseria turncoats, namely Charles Luciano and Vito Genovese—two men who would later become some of the most famous mobsters in history. Luciano, Genovese, and their followers agreed to betray Masseria and lure him to his death in exchange for full control over their own Mafia Families, which laid the foundation for the infamous modern-day "Five Families" of New York City (The American Mafia, n.d.).

For the time, Siragusa could rest easy knowing that one of his closest allies was now in charge of the largest organized crime unit in the nation, and that his enemies were all either dead or recruited. Unfortunately, this situation wasn't meant to last. In September 1931, Luciano, Genovese, Albert Anastasia, Joe Adonis, and the rest of the men who helped Maranzano win the war decided to turn on their new boss. Apparently, Maranzano's grandstanding and old-school mentality irked the younger, more progressive-minded generation of gangsters. According to Luciano, leader of their cadre, there should be no "boss of bosses," and Maranzano was not much to worship anyway. Under his orders, a crew of Jewish gangsters cornered Maranzano in his office and executed him on September 10 (The American Mafia, n.d.).

With Maranzano now dead, Siragusa was without his top ally, and without any sort of amicable connection to New York City. His position as boss of Pittsburgh was at risk to competitors, and beside that, there were likely more than a few people in New York that just wanted to see him dead. Indeed, in the weeks and months following Maranzano's murder, there appears to have been a string of executions of Maranzano allies. In 1963, mobster Joe Valachi spoke to the U.S. Senate and described the aftermath as a kind of purge of Maranzano loyalists that was not confined to New York City (Ove, 2000; Cipollini, 2023).

Along with eliminating the "boss of bosses" title, Luciano was apparently also trying to eliminate the older, conservative generation of Sicilian-born Mafia veterans. Siragusa was not spared. In fact, he appears to have been one of the first hit. Just days after Maranzano was executed, Joe Siragusa's dead body was discovered in his basement, covered in bullet wounds. According to a mob legend, the don's beloved pet parrot was repeatedly squawking "Poor Joe!" when his body was found (Ove, 2000). Pittsburgh waved goodbye to one of their shortest-lived crime bosses.

# CHAPTER 3
# THE PLAGUES OF WYLIE AVENUE

The murder of Joe Siragusa technically remains a mystery. We don't know who shot him or who gave the order, but the timing of it all makes it incredibly likely that the decision was made in New York City, not Pittsburgh. If this is true, then 1931 marks the first time that the New York City Mafia exerted direct power and authority in the Steel City.

This was not a blip on the radar; this was the way of the future. While Pittsburgh mobsters steadily grew their power through the Prohibition era, the New York mob had morphed into something uncontainable. Mafia developments at a national level began to deeply affect the bloody and violent Pittsburgh underworld, and the specter of New York would hang over the Pittsburgh Family for the next several decades. As they proved during the reign of Pittsburgh's next boss, they were the ones calling the shots.

## Bazzano and the House of Volpe

Joe Siragusa's death did very little to quell the violence in Pittsburgh. Jack Palmer, a Sicilian bootlegger who Americanized his name, was shot in the head on Wylie Avenue—which was a hub for the new incoming boss of Pittsburgh, the mild-mannered John Bazzano.

Apparently, Bazzano had been well-acquainted with Mafia old-timer Nicola Gentile from the pre-Prohibition days.

Many years earlier, under Gregorio Conti's reign, Gentile had fled the country for Sicily, but had since returned stateside. In 1931, he was openly supporting Bazzano's bid to replace Siragusa in the boss seat. With the blessing of a well-respected guy like Gentile, and the muscle to back him up, Bazzano easily claimed the Steel City throne—as unlikely as it may have seemed at the time. He wasn't outspoken, and he wasn't particularly fond of violence. He didn't even seem that ambitious. His tenure as boss, though, was a sight to behold.

Born in 1889 in the Southern Italian peninsula of Calabria, John Bazzano was the first non-Sicilian boss of Pittsburgh, and the first Calabrian to hold that much power since Conti launched the war that led to the demise of the 'Ndrangheta and the Camorra (The American Mafia, n.d.). Further details on Bazzano's history are conflicting. Some claim that he and his family had been in America since the 1890s, but it appears far more likely that he actually migrated around 1909, first living for a time in the Appalachians of West Virginia before moving to Johnstown, Pennsylvania, and finally settling in Pittsburgh.

By 1916, Bazzano was an American citizen and served his new country in the First World War, after which he returned home and opened up the Rome Café, a coffee house in the city. During his early years in Pittsburgh, he came under the wing of Nicola Gentile, who later helped him fill the void left by Joe Siragusa. But Gentile alone couldn't guarantee a peaceful transition of power. Bazzano needed strength, which he found in his alliance with the powerful Volpe brothers—all eight of them (Mullen, 2021).

Collectively, the Volpes ran the entire Neapolitan faction of the Pittsburgh Family, and operated mostly out of Turtle Creek and Wilmerding. The close alliance with Bazzano was fruitful in the early years, and most of the papers even referenced Bazzano as the direct head of the infamous Volpe operation. As we've covered, Bazzano's rise to power was pretty unlikely—he was a soft-spoken nice guy who flew under the radar whenever possible—but his close alliance with the Volpes was even more surprising. The Volpe brothers, led by the eldest John, were notorious party animals. They loved flashing their cash, buying expensive and attention-grabbing cars, and throwing endless, extravagant underworld get-togethers with Pennsylvania's biggest names and highest rollers. They lived for the gangster lifestyle.

This was in stark contrast to the quiet family man Bazzano, who preferred spending his free time with his wife and five children. That is, when he wasn't signing off on someone's death warrant. Bazzano, after all, was not a pushover despite his nice guy facade. From his beautiful stone-brick mansion in the luxurious Mount Lebanon neighborhood, the Calabrian boss was still the one calling the shots, and his patience only stretched so far. That much was obvious from how his relationship with the Volpes ultimately ended.

The first members of the large Volpe family first began arriving in the United States from Naples in the early years of the 1900s (Mellon, n.d.). The first was Ignazio, the family patriarch and father to the eight Volpe brothers. John, the eldest son, arrived several years later and joined his father in Pittsburgh. Then finally, John's younger brothers, as well as his mother, joined them. By 1915, the entire Volpe clan was in Pittsburgh. They settled in the Wilmerding borough in Allegheny County where they opened up a family-run grape and winery business. Ignazio very likely had organized crime connection back home in Naples, and his sons followed his path in America—starting with John, who likely inducted his younger brothers as well. In the years approaching Prohibition, the Volpes were not worth much consideration, but when the Volstead Act created an entirely new illegal booze market, the Volpes were well-prepared to capitalize on it with their expertise in the wine business. Unlike Conti, they didn't try to cut and run, booking it back to Italy. Instead, they firmly implanted themselves into the Prohibition-era economy, which is where the family made their real fortunes.

Under the reigns of Sal Calderone, Stefano Monastero, and Joe Siragusa, the Volpes steadily grew their power. They accumulated a lot of political power in particular, schmoozing up to state senators, council members, and the like. After all, if you wanted a party with booze and women, the Volpes were the guys to go to, and American politicians were certainly not immune to these vices. Having these kinds of political connections were important for the Volpes, who were always seeming to get into trouble.

John, in particular, was known to be violent and steadily more aggressive the drunker he was. He had been arrested numerous times over the years leading up to John Bazzano's ascension in 1931, usually for assault. He had attacked and brutalized police officers as well as newsmen who were always trying to get snapshots of the notorious socialite mobster. He was even known to violently confront the editors of Pennsylvania newspapers that published unflattering stories about his escapades (Mellon, n.d.). In all cases, he was arrested. In most he was also charged, but exactly zero resulted in a conviction. John's ego was about as large as Pittsburgh itself, and the man had laughed in the face of justice so many times that he probably felt like he owned the county courthouse. After all, the judges there followed his orders as much as any of his bartenders or smugglers.

The Volpes weren't just protected by their political and legal stooges; they also had a kind of cult following among the locals in Wilmerding and the surrounding area. They were well-loved in their home neighborhoods, and were known as benefactors for providing well-paying jobs at a time when most Americans couldn't afford their rent. The Great Depression struck the United States in 1929, and Pittsburgh was certainly not spared. While most Americans were just barely scraping by, the Volpes were living large, driving around in luxury cars, and wearing expensive suits. That was never a source of resentment though, as the Volpes were always generous with their money, and would often lend their help to the poor Italians in their communities.

They were also, apparently, fierce protectors of the less fortunate. One of the more sensational stories of the Volpes' heroics involved members of the Ku Klux Klan (KKK), a violent white supremacist group that operated in the United States from the 1860s all the way up to the 1960s, and even in the early 1980s. Today, they have faded into irrelevance, but in the 1930s, they were a dreadful force across the American South, targeting all non-white and non-Protestant citizens. Between 1920 and the late 1940s, they were also highly active in Pennsylvania, and Italian immigrants—who were almost invariably Catholic—were often terrorized by the white-hooded racists. One night, a couple of inept and unlucky Klansmen decided to burn a cross on a hill in the Italian neighborhood in Wilmerding—Volpe territory. Then, it happened again. The third time, the Volpes were ready for them. The bodies of the two KKK members were found in the morning, tortured and beaten. Other stories of their philanthropic guardianship of the people ensured that the Volpe's underworld image remained pristine (Mellon, n.d.).

Among the brothers, John was unquestionably the top guy. James and Arthur were two of his closest allies and partners, and the two of them held their own fair share of influence in Wilmerding, and even in Pittsburgh's core. Louis, another younger brother, was also an important player, but in the early 1930s, it appears he was in and out of the county jail on charges related to his family's bootlegging. Louis may have been taken down, but the others were still going strong, even in the face of increased competition within Wilmerding from both outside and local moonshiners.

The year 1932 marked a turning point for the House of Volpe. Aside from the fact that young Chester had recently died in a car accident, leaving only seven remaining brothers, John was also becoming more aggressive in his territorial grabs. He started jacking up both the cost of the products that he sold to the speakeasies and the protection fees he extorted them for. He and his brothers also began pushing into territory that was not theirs to take. This included Hill District, the traditional core of the Pittsburgh Mafia and Bazzano's home territory. Luigi Lamendola, the old power-hungry Chicago bootlegger, made a similar mistake years prior and suffered the consequences.

By summer of 1932, the Volpes seemed to have barely a care in the world. They had received little pushback since encroaching into land outside Wilmerding, and had even begun using John Bazzano's own coffee shop, the Rome Café at 704 Wylie Avenue, as their own personal meeting spot. Perhaps they believed they had the right, considering their alliance with Bazzano, or perhaps they thought the mild-mannered Calabrian would simply let them do whatever they want. Whatever the case, the Volpes had been testing the don's patience for months. In addition to their flagrant and unsanctioned expansion, they were also simply drawing too much attention to the Family. It seemed like new articles were being published almost daily directly naming the Volpes and implicating them in all manner of criminal dealings. For Bazzano, who valued discretion immensely, this was more than a mild nuisance. When the brothers unilaterally decided to force their way into the North Side rackets, their fates were sealed. Bazzano gave the order to have them slaughtered.

In one swift stroke, Bazzano crippled the leadership of the mighty Volpe bootlegging empire. On the morning of July 29, 1932, John Volpe strolled into John Bazzano's Rome Café, where his two brothers James and Arthur had been waiting for him. With the three brothers were about five or six of their associates, as well as Santo Bazzano, the Pittsburgh don's brother, who was tending the bar. A little past noon, a vehicle pulled up just down the street from the café, and three men armed with concealed pistols emerged. One of these men was later confirmed to be Giuseppe Spinelli, a former associate of the Volpes. John, who was standing outside the café at the time, saw the three suspicious looking men approaching. When they reached for their weapons, the elder brother ran, trying to escape to the safety of his bulletproof Cadillac. Before he could get inside, the assailants shot him several times. Hilariously, John then stumbled down the street covered in blood and collapsed into the arms of a horrified female bystander, causing her to faint and sending them both tumbling to the ground. After John was taken care of, the men entered the café and started blasting. James was hit three times in the face as he was trying to make his breakaway and Arthur, somehow oblivious to the situation unfolding, was hit twice in the back of the head as he sat facing the back wall of the café. Coincidentally, Santo Bazzano just happened to duck behind the counter before the shooting started, leaving him perfectly unharmed (Mullen, 2021; Mellon, n.d.; The American Mafia, n.d.).

## The Mafia Commission

The triple murder of the elder Volpe brothers shook the entire Western Pennsylvania underworld to its core. The Volpes were not minor players, and the decision must have come from high up. Just like when Lamendola was murdered, everyone already knew who gave the order as soon as the news broke. In the immediate aftermath of the dramatic shootout on Wylie Avenue, both John and his brother Santo were called in for questioning by the police, but both of them repeated the same story: They would never hurt John or James or Arthur—the Volpes and the Bazzanos were dear friends. Santo and the don were just as broken up about their deaths as Louis or any of the other remaining Volpe brothers, or so they claimed. The surviving Volpes, who all went into hiding after the shooting, felt differently about the situation. In any case, the Bazzanos were released by police and not charged for the murders.

His story about mourning the loss of the Volpes may have been enough to get the police off his back, but it didn't fly in the underworld. The police were, in fact, the least of his problems. The Volpe murders angered a lot of people, and not just in Pennsylvania. The Volpes had a large reach and plenty of friends, and John's death in particular presented cash flow problems for gangsters as far away as Ohio, Illinois, and New York. Bazzano may have felt like he had eliminated his number one problem, but not eliminating all the Volpe brothers proved to be a critical mistake. At least two of the surviving brothers (Louis was still in jail) fled to New York City.

There, in the heart of the new national Mafia administration led by Charles "Lucky" Luciano, they planned to get revenge on the Pittsburgh boss. When Sal Maranzano was murdered in 1931 and supplanted by Luciano after the conclusion of the Castellammarese War, sweeping changes were made to how the national Mafia conducted business—in New York City and elsewhere. As explained in Chapter 2, they implemented the infamous Five Families structure, whereby Luciano, Vincent Mangano, and others were given control of their own Family.

The other important innovation was the Mafia Commission, which was the brainchild of Luciano himself. The idea behind the Commission was that the Mafia should no longer be ruled by a self-styled "boss of bosses," which always led to resentment, infighting, and violent power-grabs. This would be replaced by a Commission, whose chairmen would represent the various Mafia Families from across the nation. This panel of senior gangsters would now be the ultimate power in the Mafia. The chairmen were all considered to be equals under this power-sharing system, with no single, supreme head of the organization. The most influential bosses would have seats on the Commission, while less relevant Families would instead be represented by one of their more powerful allies. It would be these men who would now settle the disputes and feuds between NYC Families, as well as those across the nation. Their word was to be considered final in all underworld matters. Most importantly, in order to deter power-grabs and civil wars, made men were agreed to be off-limits for assassinations *unless* the Mafia Commission voted and gave their express consent to eliminate one of their own. Unfortunately, the dead Volpe brothers were indeed made guys, and Bazzano sought no such consent.

When the surviving Volpe brothers arrived in New York, they spoke with several members of the Commission to explain the situation with the Pittsburgh boss. Several New York bigshots, including Luciano's underboss (and future boss) Vito Genovese, were outraged at the unsanctioned slayings of John, James, and Arthur—all of whom worked closely with Genovese. Bazzano had powerful backers in New York City as well, most notably boss Vincent Mangano and his underboss Albert Anastasia, but even those two could not abide by Bazzano's unilateral decision to wipe out three important (and profitable) bootleggers. The other Commission chairmen seemed either to have agreed, or simply acquiesced under pressure from Vito Genovese, who was prepared to go to war over the hits. Even before he was boss, Genovese held immense sway over mob politics, and with Luciano in his corner, there was no question that Bazzano was going to have to answer for what he did.

It's not clear why Bazzano decided to murder the Volpes without approval in the first place. The most likely answer is that Bazzano simply didn't take the Mafia Commission seriously in 1932. Few could blame him. It was, after all, a very new innovation, and there had not been anything like it before in the history of the Italian-American mob. Plus, although the New York Families had proved that they could hit Pittsburgh if they wanted to when they eliminated Joe SIragusa, Pittsburgh was still John Bazzano's territory, and he may have genuinely believed that the decision was his alone to make. The Mafia Commission had not yet even really proved that it was an effective apparatus for maintaining order and guiding the national Mafia. Given all this, it's not all that surprising that Bazzano didn't bother to seek approval for the Wylie Avenue Massacre.

Unfortunately for him, this presented the perfect opportunity for the Commission to demonstrate their authority to everyone, and to prove that they were not just a figurehead organization. Bazzano was going to be their sacrificial lamb. A short while after the police initially questioned John and Santo Bazzano in the shootings, they returned to speak with them again. Arriving at John's house, police were greeted instead by his wife, who told them that her husband wasn't home. In fact, he had been gone for a few days. The police didn't know where he was, nor did his wife. She assumed he was away on business, which was exactly untrue. As it turned out, the Pittsburgh don had been ordered to appear before the Commission in New York City, along with Joe Tito and Giuseppe Spinelli, one of the Volpe shooters. The three of them left Pittsburgh for New York on August 4. Accounts differ on what exactly took place upon their immediate arrival, but it appears that both Spinelli and Tito were allowed to leave and return to Pittsburgh in short order. The don, however, was told to stay behind. The New York bosses knew that neither Spinelli nor Tito would have been the ones that gave the order, and so Bazzano was forced to justify what he had done (The American Mafia, n.d.).

Evidently, he was less than convincing. Some sources claim that Bazzano admitted to the entire thing, and was willing to accept the Commission's determination. Others claim that Bazzano tried to appeal to the more bigoted mobsters, saying the Neapolitans like the Volpes were gaining too much power in both Pittsburgh and New York, and that they should band together to eliminate the Camorra remnants. Whatever the case, Bazzano's fate was almost certainly decided well before he traveled to New York.

On August 8, two days after he failed to absolve himself in front of the Commission and four days after he left Pittsburgh, John Bazzano's body was discovered by a local Brooklyn teen. Stuffed into a large, bloody bag in a pile of garbage, the Pittsburgh boss had severe rope burns across his throat and neck, and his hand and feet were bound together. For good measure, he was also stabbed several dozen times. By August 11, the police had identified the body as missing Pittsburgh businessman John Bazzano. Several arrests were made in the ensuing investigation, but no one was ever charged. For a time, there was fear that the Commission also gave the nod to eliminate the boss of the Cleveland Family, Frank Milano, because he was close friends with Bazzano, and Vito Genovese suspected him of collaborating in the Volpe shooting, but nothing ever came of that (Mellon, n.d.)

The life of John Bazzano was the only one the Commission needed to take to prove their point. From this point forward, they would be a significant force in governing the Mafia from the Atlantic coast to the Pacific. The Pittsburgh Family, which was now without a boss yet again, would feel the power emanating from New York for decades to come.

# CHAPTER 4

## THE STEEL CITY MAFIA

The Bazzano years were the last of the ultraviolent Prohibition era in Western Pennsylvania. By the time the dramatic Wylie Avenue massacre happened, Prohibition was already on its last legs. The law was deeply unpopular, the government was losing tax revenue, and millions were being spent to fund the Bureau of Prohibition, which was deeply ineffective and bloated with bureaucracy. The legislation itself simply didn't work. Americans had proved that they were unwilling to give up alcohol. By the 1930s, more American adults were drinking alcohol than in the years prior to its enforcement. Gangsters were flooding the streets of every major city with cheap booze, and hardly anyone had any moral objection to breaking this particular law.

Perhaps worst of all, Prohibition was transforming the American Mafia into a powerhouse of a criminal organization. The profits were so great that the generational wealth being created would be felt for the next several decades. Rum-running mobsters used their new wealth to establish more successful business ventures, purchase political connections, and cement themselves in the top echelon of the underworld. Still, when America heard that legal alcohol was on its way back, the Mafia entered yet another new stage, in which they would have to return to their old money-making schemes—many of which they had abandoned with the dawn of Prohibition. For the Pittsburgh Family in particular, this new stage also included preparing for the long tenure of a new, soon-to-be legendary boss.

## **Old Habits, New Don**

With the passing of Bazzano, so too passed the most violent period of the Pittsburgh Mafia to date. It was capped off with the triple homicide the Volpe brothers and the subsequent brutal murder of their killer. The span between 1920 and 1933 was an utterly chaotic time in which the Family never had a long-lasting boss, and so Bazzano's short tenure was just par for the course. Having to adjust to his absence was not nearly as daunting as having to adjust to the repeal of the Volstead Act, which closely coincided with the don's death. By the end of 1933, alcohol was once again legal for manufacture and consumption, allowing the government to dominate the market that the gangsters had a decade-long monopoly over (Ove, 2000; Mullen, 2021; Jamika, 2020). At first, this was a massive blow to not just Mafia Families in America's major cities, but also to Black, Irish, and Jewish gangs as well. The entire underworld shifted in 1920 to accommodate the new thirst for illegal liquor, so when that avenue was closed, new ones needed to be opened.

Without their number one source of income, the mob had to return to their old habits: Prostitution, loan sharking, and good old extortion were king once again. The Pittsburgh Family, in particular, leaned very heavily into illegal gambling once Prohibition was ended—an industry which future bosses would profit greatly from. Ironically, the Pittsburgh Family actually fared quite well in the aftermath. Where other Families were struggling to adjust to post-bootlegging America, the Pittsburgh Family was becoming more cohesive, powerful, and deadly.

In the immediate wake of John Bazzano's murder, it's not clear who took control of daily operations in Pittsburgh. It's possible that for a brief period, there was no one calling the shots in the Steel City because the Mafia Commission had made it clear that Pittsburgh had become a "trouble child." Once the dust settled though, it was Vincenzo "James" Capizzi that was on the top of the pile. His is perhaps one of the foggiest reigns of any of the Pittsburgh bosses. Like many previous bosses, Capizzi was a grocer by trade, something he brought with him from his hometown of Villarosa in Sicily. In Pittsburgh's North End, he also held a lot of influence with the local Sicilians.

Outside of this, not very much is known about Capizzi or how he ran the Family. He was undoubtedly well-connected, and he nominally held the title of "boss" by the end of 1932. However, at best, he was sharing power with his underboss, Frank Amato. Amato was also very well-connected, and had a close working relationship with New York's Vito Genovese—a fellow ambitious Neapolitan who would eventually become the nation's premier crime boss. Frank Amato was destined to become boss one day, and in the grand scheme of things, Vincenzo Capizzi served mostly as a transitional boss between the chaos of Bazzano and the steadiness of Amato.

After Gregorio Conti won the Neapolitan War of 1916-17, most of the non-Sicilian gangs were absorbed into the broader Mafia umbrella of Pittsburgh. There was still factionalism, but for the most part, the Pittsburgh don was regarded as the leader of all Italian crime syndicates in the city. Once Prohibition hit, and people got the sense that anyone could get rich as long as they had some yeast and a couple stills, the Pittsburgh underworld once again became fractured. Especially after 1925, there was infighting and splinter groups that broke off from the main Mafia network.

Once the Wild West age was over and Prohibition was in the rearview mirror, it was once again time to reign in the disparate gangs and reassert the Mafia's control over Pittsburgh organized crime. With Capizzi and Amato at the helm, Pittsburgh underwent another amalgamation of smaller crews under their authority. Over the course of the next five years, the Family steadily grew in power, and began breaking into both the legal and illegal gambling markets.

Capizzi lasted just shy of six years in power. It certainly wasn't a legendary reign by any means, but by the standards of Pittsburgh, this was actually quite a significant tenure. More impressive than the length of his rule, though, was the nature of his departure. He hadn't been marked for death by New York mobsters, and he wasn't gunned down in his office by angry rivals or blown up in his car with an explosive. Instead, he simply retired of his own decision in 1937, and then facilitated a peaceful transfer of power from himself to his former underboss: the new don of Pittsburgh, Frank Amato. This was a sign of the new times ahead, as Frank Amato marked a serious turning point for the Family. The transition of the Pittsburgh underworld began with Capizzi, but Amato brought unprecedented levels of stability, unity, and prosperity to his new organization. In a time where the city of Pittsburgh was undergoing massive changes (it was, at the time, one of the fastest growing cities in the entire country), it's Mafia was changing, too.

Frank Amato was a native of the town of Roccarainola, a village less than 40 kilometers northeast of Naples. This meant that, as far as the Mafia was concerned, he was a Neapolitan. It's not clear what crew Amato ran with prior to becoming boss, but it's likely that he at least had ties with the Volpe brothers, who ran the Neapolitan faction. He may have served directly under the slain John Volpe, but his "rank" is not known. Like the Volpes, Amato was also close allies with Vito Genovese, whose native town of Risigliano directly bordered Roccarainola to the south. Whether the proximity of their hometowns is what brought them so close together or not, the alliance was fruitful, and Vito Genovese was Frank Amato's official representative on the national Mafia Commission. With the support of Genovese and his New York allies, Amato moved to expand the Family's stranglehold over the gambling rackets in Allegheny and the rest of Western Pennsylvania, and to dominate the rest of the small local crews that were still calling themselves independent.

Unlike many past bosses and captains, Amato wasn't just a grocer who had illegal poker or blackjack operations on the side. He committed fully to the gambling kingpin lifestyle, and his primary legitimate business was a coin-operated machine distribution company that he founded in Pittsburgh. The company was, plainly enough, called Coin Machine Distributing. They specialized in gambling equipment, such as slot machines, but also supplied equipment like pinballs and other game machines to arcades. Surprisingly, arcades were very often connected to the Mafia at the time. Guys like Amato would often intimidate local arcade owners into buying their equipment exclusively from their distribution companies. On top of that, they would typically demand a cut of the winnings per machine. In some cases, machines were also rigged to ensure they paid out only a certain amount. Schemes like this made Amato's enterprise highly successful.

Frank Amato also introduced a slew of important mafiosi to the Pittsburgh "big time," ballooning the size of the Family and preparing it well for years of growth. Coin Machine Distributing was run by Amato, but he also enlisted the help of the notorious Mannarino brothers Gabrielo—also known as "Kelly"—and Sam. Amato also inducted the up-and-coming John LaRocca to the upper tier of the Pittsburgh Family, an organization that would one day bear his name. Needless to say, LaRocca was destined to lead the Family in the coming years. Amato's son, Frank Amato Jr., also became involved in the Family business under his father, and he ended up becoming a bigshot gambler in the city. Yet, Junior always managed to keep a low profile, a skill that he learned from his father.

Mike Genovese (no known relation to Vito in New York City), who would be a major future player in Pittsburgh, was inducted as a made man during this time as well. The young Genovese was a solid guy—he had a couple run-ins with the law early in his career through the 1930s and 40s, but he was never locked up for long and remained a very active mafioso under Amato for his entire reign. Actually, it didn't seem like Genovese was afraid of being arrested much at all. His first booking was for armed robbery in 1936, but after the US entered the Second World War, he got himself arrested repeatedly just to avoid the draft. He was successful right to the end, and his last wartime arrest was in 1945 when he was caught walking around with a pistol in Ohio. He never served a single day of combat (Hodos, 2023; The American Mafia, n.d.).

Frank Valenti was less connected directly to Pittsburgh affairs than some of the other upcoming mobsters like LaRocca, Genovese, and the Mannarino brothers, but his story served as an example of how powerful the Family would become in later years. Born in Pittsburgh, Valenti was actually something of a travelling mobster, and his exploits took him from Pennsylvania to Ohio to New York and elsewhere. While in the Steel City, Valenti participated somewhat in the tail end of the Prohibition-era smuggling industry, but really came into his own in the 1940s. In this time, he and his brother Constenze developed major connections in New York state, especially in the northern city of Rochester northeast of Buffalo. Constenze later relocated there, and began building a name for himself in the underworld of upstate New York. Later, in 1958, Constenze managed to seize control of the entire Mafia there, becoming boss of the Rochester Family (Hodos, 2023; Vallin, n.d.).

This is where Frank Valenti becomes relevant to our story, and this will be a subject for later chapters. For now, Frank Valenti was climbing the ranks of the Pittsburgh Family while expanding his chain of Italian family restaurants across Pennsylvania. With this fresh, young crew of loyal, ambitious, and influential mobsters behind him, Frank Amato was well-prepared to guide the Pittsburgh Family through what became arguably their most successful period to date. There was relatively little violence, especially compared to 1926-1933, and civil wars and betrayal were considered more harmful than beneficial.

Under Amato, the Pittsburgh crime world was also more consolidated and centralized than it had ever been. No longer were there small, regional gangs and factions that vied for control while only paying lip service to the "don" of Pittsburgh. Nearly everyone, from two-bit hustlers to large illegal casino owners, was paying tribute directly to Amato or his guys. The infighting that plagued his predecessors was put to an end, and the Family managed to mostly stay out of the local papers in the 1940s and '50s. Rather than focus on settling petty squabbles or getting revenge on rivals, everyone was focused on making money.

But, Amato's time in power wasn't just prosperous, it was also long. Reigns lasting just a few years was a trend that Amato blew out of the water, controlling the Family fully from 1937 all the way until 1956, and only stepping down due to chronic health problems. Amato peacefully retired, handed over power, and served out the rest of his life as a special mob advisor until his death in 1973 (Hodos, 2023).

## **The Rise of Big John LaRocca**

By the time Amato decided to step down, he had already decided on who he would appoint as his successor: It was one of the mobsters that he had inducted into the Family ranks during his long reign, and arguably the most consequential of the lot. In 1956, the elder Frank Amato handed over the reins to John Sebastian LaRocca. "Big John" was a very well-connected and charismatic gangster who made a name for himself in the town of New Kensington, about 20 miles outside Pittsburgh.

Following in Amato's footsteps, LaRocca was a big-time dealer of coin-operated equipment like jukeboxes, pinball machines, slot machines, and the like. He supplied several New Kensington and Pittsburgh establishments, particularly bars, nightclubs, and arcades. Outside the bounds of Pennsylvania law, LaRocca also supplied equipment to illegal casinos and gambling houses, some of which were his rackets. Gambling had become the Pittsburgh Family's number one industry since the end of Prohibition, and LaRocca was one of the key players. Amato did well to prepare LaRocca and the Family for the future, and the fact that Amato was able to retire and hand over control to a designated heir *without* provoking intra-Family rivalries and power grabs was yet another testament to the stable environment that Amato helped to create in Pittsburgh.

John S. LaRocca was born in 1901 in the village of Villarosa in Sicily—that same little town that Vincenzo Capizzi hailed from. In 1910, his family brought him to the United States and settled in Pennsylvania, where he soon took up work in the state's booming coal mining industry. His truly was a rags-to-riches story, as he did not have the privileged upbringing that many future mafiosi would have. In fact, even some of his contemporaries were already starting to enjoy the generational wealth created by their successful liquor-smuggling parents. John, though, was cut from the old school cloth, which earned the New Kensington kingpin a lot of respect as he was climbing the ranks under Frank Amato. It also influenced the way he ran his new Family. He was a no-nonsense kind of guy by all accounts, but was also forward looking. This combination is likely what led Amato to designate LaRocca as his heir, rather than the comparatively inexperienced Michael Genovese or either of the hot-headed Mannarino brothers (Hodos, 2023; The American Mafia, n.d.).

In the spirit of continuing the peaceful and stable legacy that Amato left behind, John LaRocca announced his chosen heir and successor almost immediately after becoming boss in 1956. This was a smart move. It immediately put to bed any delusions that the other capos had of taking over the Family, and also set up a clear line of succession so the Family could avoid any turmoil when it was Big John's time to retire, or if he died. The man he selected was Michael Genovese, who was about 18 years LaRocca's junior. Genovese and LaRocca were always close allies, and Genovese had played second fiddle in the new bosses' crew for years. Through the 1950s, the duo operated LaRocca and Genovese Amusements, a lucrative front business for their illegal gambling rackets.

Paul Hodos, author of *Steel City Mafia*, personally suspected that Genovese's selection as heir was also tactical (Hodos, 2023). It may have been a clever way for LaRocca to gain the favor of the younger generation of upstart mafiosi, who generally took Genovese to be their natural leader. A lot of the younger guys took their cues from Genovese, who was now closer to the boss than ever before. If this is true, then it may have been LaRocca's way of avoiding a "young turk" situation like the one that rocked the New York Mafia so many years ago. The younger mobsters, led by Lucky Luciano, forced out or murdered many of the old school leaders, who they believed were backward and refused to adapt to the new American ways. Genovese would have been only 11 or 12 at the time, but Big John was old enough to remember the carnage that resulted from insubordination.

In 1956, LaRocca began on a path that led him to becoming the most well-known mob boss in Pittsburgh history. At the time though, he still had not earned the complete trust of the powers that be, namely the New York Mafia Commission. After the Bazzano fiasco, which required a heavy-handed response, the New York bosses viewed Pittsburgh as a kind of trouble spot, where infighting and disloyalty and suspicions caused nothing but headaches. They were satisfied with the long and peaceful tenure of Frank Amato, but worried that, after his retirement, the Family could once again devolve into chaos.

However, LaRocca was determined to maintain good business, and he learned from Amato that staying out of the spotlight was of the utmost importance. He became a well-respected community businessman, operating several small and legitimate establishments like his Gas-N-Wash in New Kensington. He also secured many important political connections both at the city and state levels, which helped him to conceal his underworld empire. At his legitimate businesses, he offered the Family's younger associates steady and honest employment, which helped keep them out of trouble. With a day job that they were expected to attend, they were much less likely to cause trouble and violence within the Family or attract legal attention.

The boss developed a kind of father-figure relationship with many of Genovese's loyalists, which helped to secure his long reign. However, all of this took time. Although the Mafia Commission gave their official endorsement to LaRocca (to not do so could have sparked another power struggle), they did not allow him full control of the Family in 1956. After Amato's retirement, a panel of

Commission Chairmen, including Carlo Gambino, Frank Costello, Albert Anastasia and others, instead took direct control of the Family, dictating their decisions from across state lines (The American Mafia, n.d.).

There wasn't much Big John could do about that. The Commission had already proven they were willing and capable of taking out Pittsburgh bosses, and they had only become more powerful since 1932. The New York Families had far more made members than any other national Family. Any one of them had enough strength to wage a full-scale war against any of the other Families in America, and to win easily.

With no real recourse, John LaRocca was forced to accept the Commission's decision and once again allow the New York bosses to meddle it Pittsburgh affairs. Things would remain this way until the panel determined that the New Kensington gangster was ready to lead the Family. That moment came sooner rather than later, and by the end of the year, he was free to guide the Family as he saw fit through the tumultuous years of the late 1950s.

# CHAPTER 5

## THE LAROCCA FAMILY

After the true emergence of "Big John" Sebastian LaRocca, the Pittsburgh Mafia reached incredible heights, attaining a level of political and criminal power that previous Steel City bosses could have only dreamt of. But, along with great new opportunities came unforeseen and unprecedented challenges. LaRocca already had his work cut out for him when the Commission took control of his Family in 1956, but it didn't take long for things to get even murkier.

As we'll see, the following year was even less auspicious for the new LaRocca regime. Troubles plagued both his personal and business life, yet he still managed to establish Pittsburgh as a firm, powerful player on the national Mafia scene. He turned out to be so influential and synonymous with Pittsburgh organized crime that the Family even took his name. From that point forward, the Pittsburgh mob would be known as the LaRocca Family.

### The Road to Apalachin

Once LaRocca was granted full and unquestioned control over the Pittsburgh Mafia, he worked quickly to shore up his position against any rivals from outside or from within. He further developed the connections he had already built throughout the

1940s and branched out as well, establishing relationships with Families from coast to coast. His influence was considerable in upstate New York, particularly Rochester, and the Family even established smaller crews in other cities that were loyal to LaRocca and paid tribute back to Pittsburgh. Salvatore Marino, one of LaRocca's captains, ran the Pittsburgh crew all the way out in San Jose, California, where the Family established long-standing ties. Down in Florida, a state that LaRocca particularly loved, the Family cozied up with the Trafficante Family and had strong business relationships around Tampa Bay and Miami. LaRocca and some of his captains worked closely with the Trafficantes in several illegal, international gambling and casino rackets.

LaRocca also had a very spread out and fairly decentralized command structure, which allowed a fair amount of independence for his underlings. This was not uncommon in other Mafia structures in the country. Typically, capos would control their own territory and run their own crews, while their boss still had the final say and collected a certain amount of money from all of the crews' endeavors. But, in Western Pennsylvania, this system of "local lords" was broader and more sophisticated. There were many semi-independent crews scattered all across the state, some even approaching Philadelphia territory, that functioned as independent organizations, yet still paid tribute to the core LaRocca crew and were obligated to follow commands emanating from Pittsburgh. Localities like Altoona, Wheeling, Johnstown, and Youngstown, Ohio, all had distinct crews that could still do business as they pleased, but when it came to down to brass tacks, LaRocca was the voice of authority.

This style of leadership worked well to help insulate LaRocca from state and federal law enforcement. He was never the one to hand any direct orders to the street level guys; there was always a complex web of command that delegated and handed down edicts. Local associates would all report to the made guy that ran their crew (typically a LaRocca Family soldier), who would then report to their local captain—like Joe Regino, who ran Johnstown, or the Mannarinos out in Westmoreland county. Each of these men would then answer to the underboss, Michael Genovese, who was most people's link to LaRocca himself. In the days before government RICO charges, it was much more difficult to prosecute someone who they couldn't prove was directly involved in organized crime, so by having a line of buffers a mile long, LaRocca was able to keep himself secured from any charges his subordinates caught.

In this pyramid of leadership, LaRocca was undoubtedly on top, but even he had to answer to the chairmen of the Mafia Commission in New York—an organization to which his only access was through his representatives, the Genovese Family. As they did with most other Families across the country, the Commission reserved the right to determine when other crews could open their books to recruit new members. So, if the Pittsburgh Family ever wanted to expand, they would need to reach out to their Commission representative for permission, who in this case was Vito Genovese (as of 1957). There were likely many reasons for this, but the most obvious is that the New York Families wanted to control membership for the smaller Families to prevent them from becoming powerful enough to challenge New York authority.

While LaRocca could not determine when new blood was brought into his Family, he did decide *who* was inducted, and with this power he almost exclusively recruited blood relatives of already made men. He correctly believed that his soldiers and capos would be less likely to turn on each other the more familial connections there were between them. Unfortunately, the opportunities given to him to expand the Family were few and far between, so Big John had to make the most of what he had. Luckily for him, he had a lot of important friends to call on.

The political connections that LaRocca furnished through the 1950s did much to reinforce the strength of his admittedly small Family. They also very likely prevented the boss from being sent back to Italy and killing his reign in the crib. When Frank Amato retired in 1956, state and federal law enforcement became convinced that LaRocca was the man chosen to replace him, and they immediately tried to move against him. The U.S. Immigration Service was directed to try to have the new don deported back to his home country of Italy on account of the criminal history that he built up during his youth. It was a bald-faced attempt to cause unrest in the Pittsburgh underworld, and it almost certainly would have worked were it not for the interference of the top politician in the entire state. As LaRocca's deportation was being processed, the Governor of Pennsylvania himself, John Fine, stepped in and issued a blanket pardon for all of John LaRocca's past crimes that the Immigration Service cited as grounds for banishment (Hodos, 2023). And, by that twist of fate, LaRocca's deportation was quashed immediately, and his future in the United States was secured, ensuring that the Pennsylvania government would be dealing with him for decades to come.

Aside from politicians, LaRocca also had powerful criminal allies in Pennsylvania, the Midwest, the West Coast, and elsewhere. He developed a close alliance with Eastern Pennsylvania gangster Angelo Bruno, so when he became boss of Philadelphia in 1959, peace and cooperation between the two largest Pennsylvania Families was assured. Nick Civella, boss of the Kansas City Mafia and key player in transforming the city of Las Vegas into a mob paradise, was also a close associate of LaRocca, and the pair often collaborated in gambling-related crime ventures. Santo Trafficante, boss of the Tampa Bay Family since 1954, was another important ally in the casino business—both in the United States and the island nation of Cuba, just off Florida's southern coast. With connections like these came connections in the entertainment industry. Like many other mobsters, he was reportedly good friends with Frank Sinatra, and was known to host the singer whenever he was in Pittsburgh. LaRocca capo Antonio Ripepi, boss of the crew in Washington County, was also close with the big Vegas entertainers, and often threw parties with guys like Sinatra and Dean Martin. All of this paints a very lovely picture for the Pittsburgh Mafia in the late 1950s, but the reality was not so rosy.

Things were developing nicely for LaRocca as he settled into his new position in early 1957, but very soon after his reign began, the entire national Mafia underworld was rocked by controversy. What followed was arguably the worst exposure the Mafia had endured since the Kefauver Committee of the early 1950s, which tried but failed to prove the existence of a nationwide Mafia syndicate. LaRocca was by no means singled out in this new calamity, but it was a sign of things to come. The Mafia, despite their best efforts, was not operating completely in the shadows anymore. The government and the FBI could not *prove* it, but they knew it was there. Long-time Director of the FBI, J. Edgar Hoover, had for years downplayed the significance of the Mafia and publicly doubted that it even existed, but this would not be the case for long. A combination of hubris, carelessness, and complacency all but pulled the curtain back on the entire Mafia in front of the eager eyes of the American public, and while LaRocca wasn't the star of this drama, his face was certainly on the poster.

In November 1957, a very high-level meeting was called between the national Mafia leadership. The force behind the meeting was the newly ascendant Vito Genovese, who had recently claimed the position of boss in Lucky Luciano's former Family. Earlier that year, Vito had staged a failed hit on his own boss, Frank Costello. This was no surprise. With Costello gone, Vito would be next in line to the throne. Besides that, plenty of people wanted Costello out of the picture anyway. The boss caused mass embarrassment to the Mafia after the televised Kefauver Committee hearings, which caught the Luciano boss on camera literally trembling under questioning. The hit ultimately failed, despite Costello being shot in the head, but it was enough for the old timer to retire and let Vito take over.

Unfortunately, Costello did still have some friends in New York that respected him, not least of all was Albert Anastasia, boss of the Mangano (later Gambino) Family. To eliminate the last vestige of potential opposition to him, Genovese also ordered Anastasia to be killed, and this one was a success. In late October, Anastasia was gunned down as he sat waiting in a barbershop. Carlo Gambino, an ally of Vito Genovese, then took over the Mangano Family. He replaced his biggest threat with a close friend, securing his seat of power in New York City. The meeting he called in 1957 was for the purpose of cementing this power.

The meeting was set to take place on November 14 at the mansion estate of Joe Barbara, a well-respected capo of the Magaddino Family of Buffalo. Barbara lived in Apalachin, a small town in upstate New York, about a three-hour drive from the core of NYC. Having the meeting take place outside the city was likely strategic, giving Vito Genovese's message a more "nationwide" tint. For the most part, the meeting was simply used for Vito to grandstand and assert himself as the new top dog: the unofficial "boss of bosses," a title that Vito's former boss had eliminated altogether to prevent exactly these kinds of power grabs. Much of the meeting was symbolic, but there was actual Mafia business that needed to be discussed, and for that, John LaRocca needed to be present. In fact, high-ranking made men from Families all across the nation were in attendance, including from each of New York's Five Families. Bosses or Family representatives came from Scranton, Philadelphia, New Jersey, Texas, California, Kansas City, Buffalo, and elsewhere. With well over 100 made men in attendance, the Apalachin Meeting, as it came to be called, is likely the single largest criminal gathering in Mafia history (Hodos, 2023).

There were several matters of business slated for Genovese and Barbara's guests to discuss, but those most relevant to the LaRocca Family pertained to the nationwide gambling operations. Narcotics was a fast-growing industry at the time, but many of the old school bosses at the time, LaRocca included, scorned the use of drugs and prohibited most of their men from dealing them, particularly heroin and cocaine. Gambling was a much safer, more reliable, and less morally questionable foundation to build an empire. Plus, with the city of Las Vegas growing more accommodating to mob business by the year, casinos and poker chips were more treasured at the time than white powder. To prepare for increased investment in the industry, the bosses at Apalachin discussed a plan to jointly operate a series of hotels and use them almost exclusively for laundering gambling profits. For his part, John LaRocca and the Pittsburgh Mafia agreed to contribute by funding the construction of at least two hotels in Pennsylvania to be used for this purpose. The Phoenix (later renamed "Sunrise"), an establishment run by Michael Genovese, was believed to have also been used for this scheme (Hodos, 2023).

Before the historic summit at Apalachin could conclude, sheer luck intervened: What Vito Genovese wanted to be his ultimate power move turned into the biggest calamity in recent mob memory. As it turned out, some police officers had been tailing Joe Barbara's son at the time, and they noticed that he had reserved a large number of rooms at a local hotel, none of which were under the actual guests' names. This made upstate New York law enforcement suspicious, but the real nail in the coffin was when a few local officers happened across Barbara's estate and noticed a packed parking lot filled with luxury cars, many from out of state. This was reported, and given the fact that Barbara was a known mafioso and everyone suspected foul play, it wasn't long before cops were swarming the Apalachin estate. Once an expedited warrant was secured, the police were given the order to storm the estate and begin making arrests. When they burst into the mansion, it sent the mob bosses inside into a panic. Some surrendered after trying to ditch their wallets or weapons, while others tried their luck at running. Most of the men that tried to make an escape were hilariously out of shape and were caught shortly afterward, desperately shambling through the snowy woods behind Barbara's property.

Amazingly, although police noted that LaRocca was in attendance, he managed to avoid arrest completely. It's not clear how he managed this, but his underlings weren't so lucky. LaRocca attended Apalachin with two of his most important capos, Michael Genovese and Gabriel "Kelly" Mannarino, both of whom were detained and questioned by police while trying to make a getaway in their car.

The fallout from Apalachin was disastrous. The huge arrest set off alarms for both federal and state law enforcements across the country. Even Washington, D.C. noticed, and the Senate began preparing to have some of the men apprehended at Apalachin brought in to testify before a racketeering committee, once again exposing some of the top gangsters in the nation to the American government and public. Worst of all, FBI Director Hoover was finally forced to admit that the Italian-American Mafia was a real and genuine threat to American society. Some theories suggest that Hoover was a frequent patron of mob businesses, particularly their gambling and prostitution rackets, which could explain his years-long hesitance to use the FBI against the Mafia (The American Mafia, n.d.). Whatever the reason was, it didn't matter anymore. To continue claiming the Mafia did not exist would have been career suicide, and his FBI now had a clear mandate to crusade against Italian-American organized crime.

After the ill-fated Apalachin gathering, John LaRocca had his work cut out for him as the boss. He went back to Pennsylvania doubtful as to whether his political connections would continue to hold up under the new, intense federal scrutiny that the calamity in New York was sure to bring. This was the beginning of a new era where no Mafia Family anywhere could skate by without major federal observation anymore. The remainder of the 1950s were not shaping up to be great years for LaRocca, and as we'll see shortly, there was more than one federal government that he was concerned about.

## **Cops, Casinos, and Communists**

In the immediate post-Apalachin period, Mafia Families had to be considerably more careful about their criminal activity. And yet, the cash would not stop flowing. That, after all, was the entire point of the Mafia. Much like several of the Midwest Families, including Chicago and Kansas City, the LaRocca Family started leaning even harder into their gambling rackets after 1957.

In this realm, the Mannarino brothers were going to be important actors, as they had long been heavy hitters in the local gambling economy in New Kensington, a place LaRocca also claimed territory. Kelly and his brother Sam were essentially local bosses in the city, and very little got done without their say-so. They had a tight grip over a wide, profitable, and deeply sophisticated gambling network, and personally operated at least one large illegal casino within New Kensington. The brothers even operated a special bussing route that would drive around picking up gamblers around the city and drop them off at the Mannarino's gambling house in the New Kensington core.

As always, LaRocca took a cut from all of their gambling operations, but the Mannarinos treated their casino like their own personal

ATM. Sam and Kelly would reportedly often waltz through the front door as they were passing by, demand that the cashier hand over some amount of cash, then walk right out and hit the town—their entire night paid for by their gamblers. It was sloppy, but at the time, it was safe. The Mannarinos operated this way in New Kensington for years, and government memoranda from the 1960s even claim that Raymond Gardlock, the Mayor of New Kensington from the early 1950s through to the 1960s, was effectively a Mannarino employee and had been on their payroll for years, along with a significant portion of the city council. In fact, Joe Merola, an associate of the Mannarinos, was once ordered by Kelly to place recording devices in town council meetings so he and Sam could review their agenda afterward (United States Government, 1961).

Pennsylvania wasn't the only place the LaRoccas made money from gambling. In the late 1950s, Las Vegas was becoming all the rage, and Mafia legends like Bugsy Siegel and Meyer Lansky had done a lot to make the city more amenable to Mafia influence. Using cash investments from the Teamsters Labor Union's pension fund, many of the city's most popular casinos came under the control of Mafia Families based in Chicago, New York, Cleveland, Pittsburgh, Kansas City, and elsewhere. Pittsburgh's ties to the Vegas scene were more tenuous than other Families, but they maintained a steady presence in the city for several years.

Milt Jaffe was an important figure here, and served as LaRocca's tether to Vegas, as well as to their partners in Chicago and Cleveland. When the Stardust Casino opened in 1958, Jaffe was sent by LaRocca to be his official representative in the establishment. The Stardust, which would later be run by the legendary Frank

"Lefty" Rosenthal (the inspiration for Martin Scorsese's mob classic *Casino*), was an important business interest for the LaRoccas, and it served as their Las Vegas "headquarters," but the Chicago and Cleveland Families also had important stakes there (Rotenstein, 2020).

In general, mob bosses couldn't simply own casinos and take profit from them legally. Due to Nevada laws around gaming, Mafia Families "owned" casinos through a web of front men, shell companies, and "investment partner" statuses. And the money certainly wasn't going straight to them. As far as the government was concerned, the profit the mob bosses took from their casinos didn't even exist. Simply put, the Las Vegas "skimming" operation went like this:

1. An appointed mob representative would enter their casino at regular intervals with a briefcase.
2. They would proceed to the casino's counting room, where all the casino's profits were calculated *before* being officially recorded as income for tax purposes.
3. Once inside, the man would take stacks of bills right from the pile of cash, in front of security guards and money counters and casino employees, and fill his briefcase.
4. He might hand out a few generous tips, and then he'd be on his way, catching the first flight back to Chicago or Pittsburgh or wherever his boss lived, to deliver the cash.

It was just that simple. Hardly anyone cared. The casinos could report false losses on their taxes, the Mafia Families that bankrolled them were getting their cut, and the government wouldn't be coming to look for the money since they didn't know it existed. Even the money counters looked the other way because they were usually pocketing cash for themselves too. It was a great scam, and by the time the Stardust was sold off (outside of mob interests) in 1969, the LaRocca Family had siphoned many millions from their vaults (Rotenstein, 2020; Hodos, 2023).

Outside America, mob gambling interests had even more potential. Due to a combination of American gambling regulations and the corrupt government of Cuba, many mobsters viewed the Caribbean nation as a ripe location to expand into. Under dictator Fulgencio Batista, Cuba (especially the capital of Havana) was very welcoming to wealthy American tourists and businessman who treated the island like a whorehouse, and they were willing to work with crooked casino developers, whose buildings would attract American dollars. In America, the mob needed teams of lawyers to jump through hoops and navigate the bureaucratic red tape to be able to sneak into the casino business. Given how malleable the Cuban government was, and how easily their officials could be bought with bribes, it was much simpler to buy your way into Cuba's casino industry. For the LaRocca Family, their flagship establishment was the Sans Souci casino, cabaret, and nightclub in Havana. The Sans Souci was a swanky place that hosted live music and all kinds of entertainment aside from gambling. In running the casino, LaRocca enlisted the Mannarino brothers, and the trio worked closely with the Trafficante Family, who had deep ties in Cuba. It was a very profitable venture.

However, problems with the Sans Souci, and with Cuba in general, began to arise in the latter half of the 1950s. Years earlier, the several

Mafia-run casinos introduced a game called Razzle to their establishments. Razzle was a highly predator chance game that was clearly designed to trick drunk or ignorant American tourists by using overly complicated and deceptive odds calculations. The game ended up being a massive success for the Sans Souci and other casinos in the city, but it didn't leave players happy.

After a few years, it had upset one too many rich Americans. Tourists began routinely filing complaints with the U.S. embassy that casinos were rigging games and robbing Americans of thousands of dollars. American diplomats and politicians, the same ones who had been helping prop up Batista against the civil war that was currently raging in Cuba, started pressuring the dictator to reign in the greed of the casino moguls. Not wanting to upset the very people that were keeping him in power, Batista started a crackdown on gambling houses across the city and banned Razzle from all businesses across the island. The Sans Souci, whose income from Razzle dwarfed that of any of their other games, was hurt financially, and the LaRoccas suffered as a result.

For years, American gangsters saw Batista as the reasonable alternative to someone like Fidel Castro, leader of the revolution seeking to overthrow him. Batista was a man they could do business with. Batista's interference in the late 1950s, though, turned many mafiosi against him, and most worried that Batista would not be favorable for organized crime much longer. Some began looking for other avenues to safeguard their profits in the worst-case scenario, and the LaRoccas were among them.

In 1958, Batista was still embroiled in a bloody armed struggle against the communist revolutionaries of Castro and his top lieutenant, Ernesto "Che" Guevara. Although Castro openly criticized American involvement in the Cuban economy, some still believed he could make a potential ally. Nearing the end of the year, the rebels were making significant gains and were expected to enter the capital of Havana before long. Some, like the Mannarino brothers, saw the writing on the wall. They knew Batista wasn't long for this world, and they instead threw their lot in with Castro, desperately wanting to get in his good graces before he seized the country and evicted all the American businessmen. To this end, the Mannarinos concocted a stunningly audacious plot, one which came right off the heels of the disastrous Apalachin Meeting that drew the nation's attention to the Mafia.

# CHAPTER 6

# DAMAGE CONTROL

In the late 1950s, although the Family was stable and cash was coming in at a steadily growing pace, the situation in Pittsburgh had started to look grim once again. The visibility of Italian-American organized crime was at an all-time high, despite the fact that the rowdy and violent Wild West days of the Prohibition era were long gone. Having a vast network of Families all linked to a central hub in New York City certainly had its benefits, but as the scandal at Apalachin taught them, it also had its pitfalls.

In the Steel City, LaRocca was learning what legal heat really felt like, and it evidently took a toll on his health heading into the 1960s. Mike Genovese would soon be facing his first real challenge as heir to the Pittsburgh throne. Most importantly, certain members of the Family were getting involved in schemes that they just couldn't manage.

## Trouble in Paradise

Early on the morning of October 14, 1958, a Mafia heist crew broke into a National Guard army depot in Canton, Ohio. They made off with a shipment of hundreds of weapons, including M-1 Garand rifles, Carbines, and submachine guns (United States Government,

1961; Hodos, 2023). Details surrounding the heist itself are quite sparse, but there's no doubt that the men behind it had connections to Families in Pennsylvania, New York, and Canada. Many were involved, but the weapons themselves were spoken for well in advance—Sam Mannarino apparently had his heart set on them. These were the same weapons that, months earlier, Mannarino's underling Joe Merola had met with Abe Seid to arrange a purchase for. It's not clear what role Merola had to play after the heist was successful, but his boss had some big ideas.

Stealing from the National Guard was audacious enough, even for the Mannarino brothers, but what Sam planned to do with them afterward bordered on the insane. Obviously, they couldn't just sit on military property for long, and Sam didn't even plan on keeping them in the country. Instead, he was going to smuggle them out of the US in an airplane and deliver them straight to the communist Cuban rebel under Fidel Castro. The Pittsburgh gangster wanted to get them there in time to help the rebels secure the downfall of Fulgencio Batista in their final push into Havana—the same man that the Mafia had supported for years, and who was actively being propped up by the American government. All this was for the sake of securing the future of the Sans Souci casino, one of the LaRocca Family's most profitable assets. This revenue was, apparently, worth the risk of stealing property from the American government and smuggling said property internationally to aid their enemies overseas. The Mannarinos were nothing if not committed.

Unfortunately for the Mannarinos and the entire LaRocca Family, the scheme was destined for embarrassing failure. The weapons loitered in Pennsylvania for the rest of October while Sam tried to secure an aircraft to transport the cargo. In this time, a joint FBI and Pennsylvania State task force was hunting the shipment down. With federal involvement, even Kelly and John LaRocca's statewide political connections would not be able to help them if worse came to worse. In early November, Sam had finally secured a suitable cargo aircraft, but by this time, the police and FBI were hot on their trail. On the day that everything was to be set in motion, the task force knew well in advance, and actually witnessed Mannarino's hired goons deliver the cargo truck with the weapons to Allegheny Valley airport. They then watched as the men carefully and casually loaded crates of stolen federal property into the hold of the idling airplane. The FBI very nearly botched the operation, though. When the order was finally given to move in, the men still on the airstrip were arrested easily enough, but they weren't able to stop the plane from taking off. Luckily, they were able to track it very soon after, and a government aircraft intercepted the plane and forced it to land in West Virginia before they even had a chance to refuel. The plan didn't make it even close to its destination, and the Mannarino grand plan was dead in the water.

The police did not have evidence at the time who masterminded the Cuban weapons heist, but everyone concerned immediately suspected LaRocca, Michael Genovese, and both Sam and Kelly Mannarino, which did not require stretching the imagination. Not all of the stolen weapons were accounted for when the plane was diverted and searched in West Virginia, and shortly after, task force agents raided several properties belonging to Pittsburgh gangsters, including Genovese, but the missing weapons were never recovered.

LaRocca and everyone else involved insisted to police and the FBI that they had nothing to do with Cuba or any stolen weapons from some National Guard base. Apparently, neither the pilot nor the guys arrested at the Allegheny airstrip were willing to sell out their bosses either—although, later testimonies revealed that Kelly Mannarino told an underling that the Cuba fiasco was entirely Sam's fault (United States Government, 1961). Amazingly, by the time the investigation was concluded, the Pittsburgh leadership was almost completely untouched by the scandal, and not a single indictment was handed down to any of their made guys. This was despite the fact these kinds of flagrant international crimes could have resulted in decades behind bars for the entire upper echelon of the Family.

The fact that the Family walked away as free men from the October bust probably seemed like a long-awaited stroke of good luck for the Family, but there were now more eyes on Pittsburgh than perhaps at any point in its criminal history. At the end of 1958, John LaRocca now had the fallout of both Apalachin and the Cuba scheme to deal with, and needless to say, things were getting a little hot. To make matters worse, LaRocca and the Mannarinos had exactly nothing to show for their efforts in Cuba.

Their worst fears were realized on the very last night of 1958, when Castro's news broke that a communist rebel army being led by Che Guevara was soon going to be within the Havana city limits. Castro's men had already captured other important cities in the country, like Santa Clara, and just before midnight, Batista announced he was resigning office and fleeing the country. With the dictator gone, Che Guevara's troops capturing the city unopposed was just a matter of time. Violent riots immediately broke out across the city as Mafia businessmen scrambled to empty their vaults and catch their private planes out of the country. Some were able to get out, but others weren't so lucky, and millions of dollars were left behind to be plundered. In the first early hours of 1959, a mob broke down the doors of Sans Souci and stormed through, stealing or smashing whatever they could (The American Mafia, n.d.; Hodos, 2023). The Pittsburgh Mafia had lost one of their highest earning properties, and the message sent was clear: Cuba was no longer open for Mafia business.

## The "Other" Genovese

With the FBI and Pennsylvania state police breathing down their necks, John LaRocca and Kelly Mannarino decided to take drastic measures: They skipped town, and were going to be gone until the heat died down and the Cuba fiasco was in the rearview mirror. The Pittsburgh Family was without their boss, and arguably their most powerful captain in the late 1950s, and for the first time ever, Michael Genovese stepped up to take on the role of acting boss in Big John's stead. It was time for the heir apparent to the Pittsburgh Mafia to prove that he was capable of running the Family, and he did not disappoint. In the big picture of Mafia history, Michael may only be the second most famous Genovese behind the legendary Neapolitan boss of New York, but Michael turned out to be as influential to the Mafia in Pittsburgh as Vito Genovese was to the Mafia in the big city.

It was going to be an uphill battle though, and Michael's trial as boss was the Mafia equivalent of teaching a child to swim by throwing him in the deep end. He wasn't as big a target for the feds as Big

John or the elder Mannarino brother, but they certainly knew who he was. At the Apalachin summit, Michael was caught alongside Kelly Mannarino in Kelly's car as they tried to flee with two of their associates from Scranton's Bufalino Family. From that day on, LaRocca's successor was on the FBI's long list.

A native of the East Liberty neighborhood of Pittsburgh since birth, Michael Genovese was the first American-born mobster to run the Pittsburgh Family, though he was just acting boss for now. The fact that he was a born and bred American gave him a lot of sway over younger mobster, most of whom were being born stateside by the 1950s. His personality was well-suited to tame the more rowdy youngsters—he was well spoken, and characteristically calm, providing an anchor for his more hot-headed underlings.

But, despite his level head, the man wasn't a fortress, and he proved quite unable to stand up under pressure. A few years after the dual disasters of Apalachin and Cuba, Genovese was called to testify before the Senate Labor Rackets Committee, a panel specifically designed to investigate and combat organized crime. Genovese was set to be questioned in front of none other than Robert F. Kennedy, the brother of the new President John F. Kennedy, who had been recently elected in 1961. This was a big deal for several reasons, not least of which was that Robert Kennedy was no average prosecutor—he had quickly become the most vigilant and aggressive anti-Mafia crusader in the entire nation.

The efforts of the President's brother helped usher in a new era in American politics, where organized crime took more and more of a central role in the collective American psyche. Gangsters of all stripes were likened to a plague, a spreading disease that infected cities across the country and degraded their morality. Their realm was vice—hookers, gambling, and drugs. They were also shifty, operating in the shadows and thriving in obscurity. The only way to combat this disease was exposure. If nothing else, the Senate Committees like the one that targeted Genovese at least accomplished this. At the hearing, Mike Genovese was reportedly squirming endlessly in his seat, with his eyes darting rapidly between the questioners on the Senate panel (Hodos, 2023). He was photographed nervously playing with his lips with his fingers like a child. It was an embarrassment for the LaRocca Family, and it did nothing to disprove the Senate's belief in the existence of the Mafia in Pittsburgh.

The acting boss was questioned in regard to his appearance at the Apalachin summit years earlier, as well as a number of his alleged gambling rackets, particularly the numbers game. Not much ever came of Genovese's Senate testimony, at least not right away, but it did scare the mobster enough to convince him to immediately shut down Archie's car wash and the numbers ring that he operated out of it. Aside from his childish display at the Senate, it was more or less business as usual in the Steel City. John LaRocca returned from his exile in the early 1960s and retook control of his Family, but he ruled with a newfound respect for his appointed heir.

Speedbumps aside, Mike Genovese presided over a peaceful and still-profitable period in the Family's history, and during this time, he cemented his claim to the boss position. It was easy for him to avoid making enemies, as he was characteristically polite, modest, and never gave the impression of being power-hungry or tyrannical. None of LaRocca's other capos revolted against

Genovese, who effectively oversaw the operations of Joe Sica in Wilmerding, Antonio Ripepi in the southwest, Frank Rosa and Joe Regino in Allegheny County, and the powerful Mannarino brothers of New Kensington. Even Sal Marino, LaRocca's lieutenant out in San Jose, was reporting loyally to Genovese. LaRocca now knew that he had made the right decision. Genovese continued to serve as acting boss whenever the need arose, and it arose a lot. LaRocca and Joe Regino apparently enjoyed vacationing in Florida for months at a time every single winter (Hodos, 2023).

Michael Genovese's ascent to this kind of position was far from a sure thing. He was not an educated man in the traditional sense, and quit school before he was able to complete the ninth grade. There doesn't appear to have been any evidence of strong Mafia ties in the Genovese family either, and neither his father Tony nor any of his older relatives were known mafiosi. Interestingly, his mother Ursula was the one with a confirmed criminal record, which she received when she was caught making moonshine in the 1930s near the end of Prohibition (Ursula, 2023).

Traditionally, the Pittsburgh Mafia had tended to prioritize working with and inducting only relatives of made guys. Plenty of outsiders made it into their ranks, but they would need to truly distinguish themselves among their mob cohorts. Michael's older brother, Felix, also worked with the Pittsburgh Mafia, and it's possible that Felix was the one that introduced his brother to the life. However, Felix was never influential enough in the Family to assure Michael's induction as a made man. The elder Genovese never advanced very far in the Family under Frank Amato or John LaRocca, largely due to his violent and unpredictable temper and his alcohol dependence. Michael, on the other hand, climbed the ranks to became a top capo and the designated Prince of Pittsburgh.

Michael became a made man under Frank Amato, and he cut his teeth in the Family by working as a bodyguard for the Mannarino brothers in New Kensington. When he became more independent and a mobster in his own right, he opened up the Genovese Cocktail Lounge in the city, which doubled as a hangout for himself and his mob associates. Later in the 1950s, he also ran the Red Eagle Club, a highly exclusive and upscale establishment befitting a high class mafioso. The youngest Genovese brother, Fiore, was enlisted to help run the Red Eagle.

From the 1960s onwards though, Genovese and his crew operated out of their hotel, the Phoenix—a nondescript location that was far less conspicuous than a fancy cocktail bar. Having been schooled by the likes of Amato and LaRocca, Genovese appreciated the value of flying under the radar. Even his home was modest, despite the large property he had. Since 1956, he lived in a converted farm property with his second wife and children (he had married his first wife years earlier, but the man was a known philanderer, and his wife soon left him with their daughters and moved to California). The original owner of the farm was apparently deeply in debt to Genovese over his chronic gambling habit, and he was forced to give up his entire property to the man in lieu of payment.

Genovese was a product of LaRocca in many ways, but the more youthful and progressive of the men had his own plans for when he took over the Family. He also ran his crew in a much different way than Big John. Like many of the older generation of mob bosses of the 1950s and 1960s, John LaRocca had a strict policy against his men dealing in narcotics. The potential profits from selling marijuana, cocaine, and heroin were very enticing, and everyone knew there was a large market that could be monopolized in Pittsburgh.

It could have been bigger than the bootlegging business during Prohibition, but there was a major difference: The police officers of the 1960s were not as easily bribed as those of the 1920s and 1930s, and the government agencies designed to combat the scourge of drugs were less bloated and far more effective than the now-defunct Bureau of Prohibition. Drugs meant big trouble from law enforcement, and it was too big of a risk for guys like LaRocca. He especially didn't want any of his guys using drugs themselves, as he was afraid of having his underlings strung out on cocaine and running their mouths about their business, or getting in trouble with the police.

Genovese, on the other hand, was far more accepting of the drug trade, and knew it presented too great an opportunity to pass on. Throughout the 1960s, Genovese got more and more involved in the narcotics business, all right under the nose of his boss. He obviously was determined to take the Family in a different direction, but his new source of income would bring as much trouble as it would profit. For now though, he was biding his time, waiting for the moment John LaRocca would hand him the keys to Pittsburgh.

# CHAPTER 7

## NEW TURF, NEW BOSSES

The late 1960s and early 1970s was a period of significant growth, but it also introduced another new set of challenges for the LaRocca Family. For the first time since the Mafia Commission had John Bazzano slaughtered in humiliating fashion, the Pittsburgh Mafia began to assert itself on a national level. Especially in the 1970s, other larger Mafia crews around the country were facing more significant legal problems than they had ever faced before, and LaRocca, Genovese, the Mannarinos, and the other Steel City captains were eager to seize on their moment of weakness.

Unfortunately, these men, as well as the entire upper tier of the Family, were also getting older in age. Health problems plagued the senior leadership, including Michael Genovese and Big John LaRocca himself. More legal problems compounded the issue. The 1970s was a time when leadership and authority needed to be asserted, both at home in Pittsburgh and elsewhere.

### The Coup of Rochester

At some point in the early 1960s, after LaRocca had returned from hiding from the fallout of Apalachin and Cuba, a member of the New York-based Genovese Family named Salvatore Granello was on the verge of setting up a very lucrative deal—or so he thought. Granello, known better as "Sally Burns," had been having several meetings over the past several weeks with Herbert "Herb" Itkin. Itkin was a well-known crooked lawyer that often worked for the Mafia. He had been involved in numerous mob schemes over the years, mostly relating to the Teamsters Union Pension Fund, as well as their casino operations in Cuba prior to Batista's downfall. Itkin had told Granello that he had the perfect opportunity for him, one which would give him and his Genovese Family associates deep access to the Teamsters Pension Fund, the same one that bankrolled the construction and refurbishment of most of the mob casinos in Las Vegas. This was a potentially massive deal on paper, as access to the fund meant access to tens of millions of dollars for various business ventures. Naturally, Granello was interested.

The Genovese soldier also wanted to get some of his other friends in on the deal, and as it happens, he was quite close with the LaRocca Family in Pennsylvania. Granello introduced Herb Itkin to John LaRocca and Kelly Mannarino, who, were eager for a potentially big new casino deal after losing the Sans Souci in Havana. Joe Sica, LaRocca's capo in Wilmerding, also got involved in the deal. Sica had likely been involved with deals brokered by Itkin before, as he had his own personal ties to the NYC Families. He was the cousin of Al D'Arco, the future acting boss of the Lucchese Family, which ran several illegal poker joints in Vegas. The Pittsburgh crew was in too deep, and they stood to profit in a big way. Unfortunately, it turned out to be another debacle.

Herb Itkin, known to the FBI as "Mr. Jerry" and to the CIA as "Agent Portio," was actually a co-operating agent of the U.S. government

(Capeci, 2015; Central Intelligence Agency, n.d.). He had been covertly compiling evidence on his mob associates for years. Previously, his information had contributed to the downfalls of criminals like Lucchese boss Tony Corallo, and the exposure of crooked New York politicians like Carmine de Sapio. The FBI knew as much about his alleged Teamsters scheme as LaRocca did, and when they finished compiling enough evidence, federal agents moved in and handed out indictments for Granello and nearly the entire upper echelon of the Pittsburgh Mafia, including LaRocca, Kelly Mannarino, Joe Sica, and Sica's son-in-law Frank Rosa. After a prolonged legal battle, the Pittsburgh crew was eventually acquitted in the case. Kelly Mannarino was targeted especially aggressively, and he wasn't fully off the hook for the bust until 1970. They remained free men at least, but Sally Burns Granello sealed his own fate by bringing Herb Itkin into their midst.

Granello was sent off to serve his sentence in Danbury Prison in Connecticut. While he was incarcerated, his son was murdered in retaliation for the FBI trap. Granello vowed revenge on whoever his son's killers were, but shortly after he was released from prison, he too was assassinated. It's unknown whether the Pittsburgh leadership had anything to do with Granello's retributory murder, but the LaRocca Family had already proven their disproportionate strength and reach considering their small size. The Family never reached more than 30 to 40 made men at any given time, which was a fraction of any of the New York City Families, but by the mid-1960s, they were no longer a crew that could be easily pushed around (Hodos, 2023).

Back in 1958, Constenze Valenti took control of the Rochester Mafia, which had long been an extension of the powerful Magaddino Family in Buffalo. Constenze was the brother of Frank Valenti, a made man in the LaRocca Family, and both of the brothers had a history in Pennsylvania as well as New York. The new Rochester boss' reign was rather short lived, and he found himself in prison soon after he took control. This wasn't a surprise, as the elder Valenti brother had been legally embattled for a couple years by that point, and when the feds concluded that he had taken the top position in the city, they moved aggressively to take him down. Traditionally, Mafia bosses would remain the official shot-caller in the Family even while incarcerated, and he would dictate orders to the acting boss from behind bars. In Rochester, there were enough disloyal elements in the long-dysfunctional Family that there was a real risk of civil war as Constenze's underlings vied for control. Many of the capos wanted to oust Constenze completely and seize power for themselves, while those loyal to the imprisoned boss tried to keep the lid on.

While this was going down in New York, Frank Valenti left Pittsburgh and went to Rochester to intervene and help his brother's loyalists maintain power in the city. Unfortunately, state police were aware of the other Valenti brother's movements, and began making moves against him as soon as he crossed state lines. The investigation into him became too intense to handle, and Frank was forced to leave New York in the midst of the power struggle. In the time since his absence, a gangster named Jake Russo eventually clawed his way to the top of the pile, and was named the new boss of Rochester. By the early 1960s, Frank was back in Pittsburgh working under John LaRocca. But Frank never forgot about the men who betrayed his brother and left him to rot in prison while they took his Family from him. It's possible LaRocca sympathized with the Valentis, or he simply saw a rare opportunity to expand his Family's power, but by 1963, he and Frank were working together to develop an incredibly daring scheme.

In 1964, with the support of John LaRocca, the Pittsburgh Mafia, and those loyal to his brother Constenze, Frank Valenti made his way back to Rochester. There, he waged a bloody and offensive war against the leadership of Jake Russo and his associates. The coup of Rochester was a success, and Frank Valenti was able to oust Russo and install himself as the new boss that same year. Frank then began a year-long purge of Russo's loyalists in the area, which only came to an end in 1970.

With the support of LaRocca and the Pittsburgh Mafia, Valenti was able to become boss of an entire Family, but his support from Pennsylvania actually went further than that. Apparently, Frank Valenti had no intention of being subservient to the Magaddino Family of Buffalo, as Rochester bosses had often been. He did not want to be the leader of a semi-independent Family. With the full backing of John LaRocca, he was able to confidently assert that the Rochester Family would no longer answer to Buffalo and would now operate as a fully independent crew.

This was a major moment for Pittsburgh. Under John LaRocca, the Family was able to stand defiantly against the Magaddinos, historically one of the most powerful Mafia Families in the country outside of New York City. The Magaddinos were in the midst of some damning legal challenges, and they just couldn't risk going to war with a Family over territory that wasn't a part of their core. On top of that, the New York City underworld was in rupture over the aggressive moves of boss Joseph Bonanno, so Magaddinos traditional allies were also too preoccupied to lend any tangible support. There were also rumors at the time that Stefano Magaddino had recently gotten very stingy with his money, and hadn't been paying what he owed to some of his guys.

In just a few short years after Frank Valenti's coup in Rochester, the powerful Magaddino Family began crumbling under the pressure from both their rivals and the law, before ultimately fading into irrelevancy. Meanwhile, the LaRocca Family and their allies were moving in to set up shop in their former territory. The Family was benefitting from remaining on the periphery of the FBI's radar, while the major Families in New York City were going through hell. But the Pittsburgh Family was not completely untouched by the new nationwide crackdown of organized crime, nor were their senior leaders getting any younger.

## **Lines of Succession**

Through the late 1950s and early 1960s, Sam Mannarino and his partner Willie Sams operated a successful coin machine business together. Sam Mannarino was considered a high-priority target within the Family, given the government's absolute belief that he was behind the plot to smuggle American weapons to Fidel Castro and the communist rebels in Cuba, but they had to wait for a tax infraction to finally take him down. In 1963, both Mannarino and Willie Sams were tried and convicted for tax fraud after being accused of falsely valuing their pinball machine profits for years. The prosecutors figured that Mannarino had knowingly avoided paying tens of thousands of dollars in taxes, and according to their findings, they were correct.

Sam Mannarino, one of the Kings of New Kensington, was on his way to a sentence behind bars. Unfortunately, the man was already in quite poor health, and his conviction only made it worse. He could no longer run any of his legal business, nor his mob rackets, and in 1964, he was forced to shut down Ken Iron and Steel, which he had run for years. Sam was eventually released in 1965 due to his failing health, and he died shortly after (Hodos, 2023; The American Mafia, n.d.). New Kensington was now down to one Mannarino brother.

Gabriel "Kelly" Mannarino was also being investigated for tax fraud in 1963, but he was ultimately acquitted while his brother received the brunt of the punishment. By 1970, he was also fully cleared of the Teamsters racketeering charges, and in fact, he was never convicted of any crimes through his long criminal career. He lived through the 1970s, and finally died in 1980 from cancer. When both the Mannarinos were gone, the LaRocca Family was without two of their most powerful—and, arguably, the highest earning—captains in Western Pennsylvania. The brothers were then replaced with Thomas "Sonny" Ciancutti, who took over most of the New Kensington and Westmoreland rackets. He didn't command anything close to the respect the Mannarinos received in their community, but he did actually end up becoming one of the most notable members in Pittsburgh Mafia history. Unfortunately, this was not for happy reasons, as we will see in later chapters.

The signs of aging didn't stop with Sam Mannarino. In mid-1968, Michael Genovese suffered two consecutive heart attacks, and very nearly died (Hodos, 2023). He spent the next months recovering in Shadyside hospital in Pittsburgh. This was potentially a major issue. LaRocca was already an old man, and Genovese was meant to be the next guy in line when he passed. Suffering such a severe health crisis set off more than a few red flags, and Genovese's rivals may have started to see him as weak. In the very least, there would be plenty of gangsters chomping at the bit to solidify themselves as Genovese's second-in-line.

Regardless, Pittsburgh's line of succession was now in question for the first time in many years. In fact, the FBI was even speculating at the time that Genovese had already been officially ruled out as boss. This, at least, appears not to have been true. He did end up recovering, and fortunately for him, both his brother Felix as well as future underboss and West Virginia gambling man Joe Pecora helped maintain Michael's rackets and stave off competition while he was in the hospital.

Health problems continued to plague the LaRocca Family heir, particularly his heart. He was either unable or unwilling to get the corrective surgery he needed until 1975, and until that time, his place in line was always challengeable. His long-awaited clean bill of health came just in time, as his brother Felix, one of his most ardent supporters, died that same year. His brother was a loss, but with his health problems behind him, Genovese once again had the confidence of John LaRocca, who reaffirmed his choice of heir. The year 1975 continued to be a very mixed one for him, though, as he was facing even more persistent legal issues. Years prior, Genovese had taken the stand in front of a grand jury under subpoena related to racketeering. He was offered certain immunities if he agreed to co-operate with the state's investigation, but when he allegedly refused, he was arrested.

After Genovese's arrest, John LaRocca somehow discovered that Tony Grosso, a bigshot in the Pittsburgh gambling rackets, had agreed to a deal with the police to inform of Michael Genovese when he had gotten arrested himself a few months earlier. It was apparently this informing that turned the law onto Genovese in the first place, and most likely led to his arrest. LaRocca was infuriated. He vowed, firstly, to allow access to Family money in order to help fund Genovese's legal team. He also vowed to have Tony Grosso murdered in prison. LaRocca set the plan in motion, but there were a few problems. Mainly, Grosso was in state custody.

For the New York City Families, having someone murdered in prison was just mundane, day-to-day business. However, the Pittsburgh Family did not have nearly as many prison connections and access as the Bonannos, Luccheses, or Gambinos did. This was mostly due to the fact that, historically, members of the Pittsburgh Mafia simply hadn't been sent to prison as often as their New York counterparts. Orchestrating a prison hit was going to be new territory for LaRocca, but he was determined. Unfortunately, the FBI caught wind of his plan and actually approached LaRocca in public about it. They told him that they knew what he was doing, and that if anything happened to Grosso, LaRocca would be arrested immediately. As a result, the Pittsburgh don was forced to kill the plan in its infancy and back down, and the bad blood between Genovese and Grosso would last for the rest of their lives.

After serving six months of his sentence, Michael Genovese was once again a free man. The arrest apparently shook Genovese, who was normally an extremely cautious man and worked hard to avoid the attention of the law. He vowed that he would never be caught so vulnerable again, and he worked diligently for the rest of his life to ensure that he never again saw the inside of a prison cell. His word paid off, and the upcoming boss remained a free man for the rest of his life.

The 1970s had other issues in store for the man, though. Before Genovese's sentencing, police speculated that there was a power struggle brewing between the heir apparent and arguably LaRocca's most powerful captain, Kelly Mannarino. The surviving Mannarino brother apparently wanted to unseat the man who LaRocca had kept waiting in reserve since the 1950s. After Genovese's trial and prison term, this rivalry likely just got hotter. But John LaRocca was a man that commanded considerable respect, both within Pittsburgh and across Pennsylvania, New York, Ohio, and elsewhere. This, more than anything else, is likely why nothing violent ever came of the Genovese-Mannarino rivalry in the 1970s. Kelly was probably waiting for LaRocca to pass before he did anything drastic, but unfortunately for him, the don ended up outliving him.

As the 1970s wore on, LaRocca was giving up more and more of his day-to-day responsibilities to Genovese as his own health deteriorated. In 1980, Kelly Mannarino died, eliminating his only real competition. John LaRocca only had a few years left in him, too. By 1982-83, Michael Genovese was boss in all but name. The decade of the 1980s would belong to him.

# CHAPTER 8
## GENOVESE ASCENDANT

For most Mafia Families in the United States, the 1980s was a bittersweet decade. It was an era of enormous drug profits as the market for cocaine boomed in New York and elsewhere. Most gangsters had never seen such easy money before. Not since the days of Prohibition were so many people dying to get their hands on their product, and willing to pay almost any price. It was also the era of RICO suits and decades-long prison sentences for organized criminals.

In 1970, Congress made into law the Racketeer Influenced and Corrupt Organization (RICO) Act. The new law, while open-ended, had the express intent of combating, and ideally eliminating, organized crime in America. There were two primary provisions within the law that were particularly damaging to Mafia Families. First, it allowed the government to seize the assets of an individual involved in a RICO case, even before they're arrested or found guilty. For decades, mobsters were able to use their ill-gotten fortunes to fund their court battles and enlist the most expensive legal teams, but with RICO, even the wealthiest mob boss could be left penniless. If any money was suspected of having been gained through organized criminal activity, it was liable to be taken.

Perhaps more importantly, it also meant that if a guy was in jail awaiting a RICO trial, then their family would be left destitute. He couldn't earn, and what money he already had wasn't accessible to his wife and children. With this kind of pressure, mobsters were much more pliable, and more than a few ended up becoming state witnesses just to protect their families.

The second important power that RICO granted was the ability to ensnare the entire chain of command in a single legal case. The point of RICO was to disrupt organized crime, which meant that they needed to be able to get at the people on top, the ones giving the orders that flowed down to those below them. Typically, mob bosses weren't the ones directly involved in committing crimes—that was the duty of their underlings. This often made it difficult to "cut the head off the snake," as a captain couldn't always be prosecuted for a crime his soldier committed, even though he may have given the order. Under RICO, if prosecutors were able to establish that a certain crime was committed in service of a larger criminal organization, then they were allowed to draw a line from the bottom to the top of the pyramid and prosecute everyone in between. So, even if a low-level soldier was charged with extortion, his boss, and his boss' boss could end up facing charges as well. Many prominent mobsters, particularly in New York City, went down this way. Aside from their increased vulnerability, some mobsters were now facing multiple life sentences for their deeds.

This was the environment of the national Mafia when Michael Genovese first started to take control of the Family from John LaRocca. It took eight years for the first federal RICO case to take place after it was signed into law in 1970. By 1985, the assault on the

Mafia was in full swing, and there was a new generation of Mafia crusaders led by men like Rudolph Giuliani, a lawyer and future mayor of New York City. Genovese shared in the successes of the decade, but he also didn't escape its tumults. But his problems were different than most of his counterparts in other states. His eventual reign in the Steel City was a significant one, but he also oversaw the near total destruction of the Family. Michael Genovese was the last relevant Mafia boss of Pittsburgh.

## **The Cleveland War**

By the time the Mannarino brothers were dead, Joey Naples had been a connected guy in the LaRocca Family for years. His home territory was Youngstown, a city in Ohio near the border of Pennsylvania, which the Mannarino brothers had long controlled. In the 1980s, Naples was the second-in-command in Youngstown behind Vincenzo "James" Prato, a made man in the LaRocca Family. Joey Naples ruled Youngstown along with Prato, but although he was powerful and respected, he was not a made man himself. Throughout the 1970s and 1980s, the Genovese Family in New York City repeatedly prevented John LaRocca from expanding his Family by restricting their induction of new members. The membership of the Pittsburgh Mafia had remained stagnant, and so guys like Joey Naples remained on the outside. Still, he made some significant decisions in his time there.

Youngstown was often considered to be the most violent and dangerous of all the LaRocca Family's territories. It had been this way for decades. In the 1960s, it became famous for its long streak of car bombings, and the town never managed to shake the reputation. Joey Naples only added to Youngstown's violent history. The mobster was notoriously brutal and brazen in his crimes. In 1979, while Kelly Mannarino was still alive, Naples was accused of setting fire to a vehicle belonging to a Youngstown city councilman. The city council, at the time, was tabling discussions on how to combat the effects of organized crime, and the general consensus was that the vehicular arson was in direct response to these discussions.

However, little came of the investigation, as corruption had been deep-seated in Youngstown. The Pittsburgh faction there, most of whom were Calabrian, had vast numbers of public servants in their pockets. City councilmen, police officials, city prosecutors, and others were eager to take money from people like Naples and James Prato. For years, it was almost assumed that if you were in a position of power in Youngstown, then you were taking mob money. Knowing this, it's no surprise Naples felt confident enough to torch a councilman's car for daring to speak out against the city's long-standing arrangement.

James Prato was born in 1907 in San Nicola, a small town in the Southern Italian peninsula of Calabria. After immigrating to the United States, he moved to Cleveland, Ohio, some time in 1930. From there, he moved to Youngstown, where his uncle Dominick Mallamo was a becoming a big shot gangster. Prato got involved in organized crime, and soon became a made man in the Pittsburgh Mafia, managing to edge his way in before their membership books were put in a chokehold by the New York Genovese Family. Joey Naples was not so lucky.

Still, the pair of them ruled Youngstown effectively for Pittsburgh, but with a place so deeply penetrated by organized crime, there was bound to be competition. The Cleveland Mafia, run by James "Jack White" Licavoli since the mid-1970s, also had a long-standing presence in the town, which they considered an extension of their home territory. For years, there was relative peace between the Pittsburgh and Cleveland factions in Youngstown. This was disrupted in the late 1970s when the Licavoli Family got involved in an all-out war with Cleveland's Irish gangs. The war quickly got out of hand, and Licavoli was forced to pull men out of Youngstown to help in Cleveland. With Licavoli's attention being pulled away, Prato and Joey Naples decided to seize on the opportunity. They launched their own war against the Cleveland Mafia in Youngstown while they were being attacked at home.

Prato and Naples were willing to throw away years of co-operation for the chance to force Cleveland out of Youngstown permanently. The Carabbia brothers, Ronnie, Charlie, and Orlando, were typically Cleveland's representatives in Youngstown. Initially, they found success in repelling the Pittsburgh faction's attacks, and even dealt a lot of blows themselves. Ultimately though, they suffered too many losses to the LaRocca Family to be able to maintain a presence in Youngstown. On Valentine's Day 1980, Cleveland mobster Rob DeCerbo was killed after being hit with several shotgun blasts through his front window as he sat watching television with his wife. This was after DeCerbo already survived a car bombing, one of Naples' signature forms of execution. Later, another Pittsburgh guy named Joe DeRose was also targeted for hits, but managed to survive (Hodos, 2023).

The death toll continued to climb until the war was an obvious victory for the LaRocca Family and for Joey Naples. It was another clear victory for the Pittsburgh Mafia, as they had secured another peripheral city as their exclusive territory, wresting it from yet another out-of-state Family. Despite this win, the LaRocca Family was still showing signs of decline in the early 1980s. Most of this had to do with dwindling membership rates (the LaRocca's may have been able to challenge Buffalo and Cleveland, but the Mafia Commission was still the ultimate authority), but it also had to do with the fact that John LaRocca himself was getting older, and much sicker.

## The New Pittsburgh Regime

In the last month of 1984, John Sebastian LaRocca, who had served as the boss of Pittsburgh since 1956, had died. At 82 years old, he died as the longest-serving and arguably most successful boss in the Steel City's history. There was a specter of uncertainty in the weeks that followed his death. LaRocca as boss was all the Pittsburgh underworld had known for decades. But, business had to go on, and real power had to exert itself.

Just as the Family's namesake had decided in the '50s, Michael Genovese took over as the don of the LaRocca Family. By this point, much of the old guard was gone. The last Mannarino brother died four years earlier, and Joe Sica fully retired from the Family shortly after he was convicted for extortion in 1978. Genovese faced very little competition rising to the top.

LaRocca had already taken several steps back from running the Family in the years before he died, but he still served as an important advisor, confidant, and revered figurehead for dealing with out-of-state Families. His death was a loss, but it was only the latest in a long series of setbacks. Fellow made man, John Verilla—an important guy in the Altoona and Johnstown branches of the Family—was put out of commission just a year earlier. His ultimate prison sentence was, if nothing else, a sign that the same legal trouble plaguing the Families of New York State had finally arrived in Pennsylvania.

Verilla worked under capo Joe Regino for years in Altoona, just a couple hours outside of Pittsburgh. This was at a time when the drug boom was really starting to be felt in Pennsylvania, and more and more mobsters were feeling the pressure to enter the market. Verilla, originally, was strictly against getting involved in narcotics, but like so many others, he gave in when he realized just how much money there was to be made from white powder. By the end of the 1970s, he was quickly becoming Altoona's resident drug baron. This development was probably nice for Verilla's pockets, but it was bad news for the LaRocca Family. Drug charges carried far less-forgiving sentences than something like gambling, which had been the signature racket of the Pittsburgh Mafia since the end of Prohibition in the 1930s.

To make this risk even worse, Verilla was not exactly a cautious man, and was notoriously ill-tempered and violent. In 1978, he was suspected of brutally murdering one of his customers, a local drug addict that he believed had been talking to the police. In 1981, convenience store owner Ernest Martz had his house shot up and his car set ablaze after Verilla discovered he was falsifying his earnings to avoid paying Verilla his full tribute. The same year, a grand jury began investigating organized crime in Altoona, a city that experienced a sharp spike in murders and arsons since Verilla took over the drug business. The situation was so bad in Altoona that the city became the site for Pennsylvania's very first RICO case. In July 1983, charges were handed down to Verilla for arson, homicide, gambling racketeering, and dealing narcotics. Two of his top lieutenants, John Caramadre and Vincent Caracciolo, also got hit with RICO charges. In 1984, all three of these men were convicted, and all received life sentences (Hodos, 2023).

The first successful RICO prosecution in the state was a significant blow for Genovese, who had only recently taken over control of the Family. After losing the command structure of Altoona (and partially Johnstown), Genovese was desperate to expand the Family to prevent them from fading into irrelevance. He would have to wait until 1986, when the Genovese Family finally gave the go-ahead to Genovese to recruit new made men. This move was likely to prevent the Pittsburgh Family from breaking away from the New York City center of command, as the Five Families were facing their own legal onslaught would scarcely have the resources to try to rein in a breakaway faction. Genovese wasted no time in recruiting—that year, he inducted Charlie Porter, Lenny Strollo, Henry Zottola, and Sonny Ciancutti into the Family. Some of these men had been waiting decades for this Even Joey Naples, the victor of the Cleveland War, finally became a made man in '86. Times were indeed changing in Pittsburgh. Around the same time, Genovese officially repealed the long-standing ban on drug trafficking, which was a remnant of the early LaRocca years by this point.

Charlie Porter and Louis Raucci became the LaRocca Family's top narcotics guys, and were the power behind Michael Genovese. Although Porter was not full-blooded Italian, he rose to a position of significant power under Genovese, and even became underboss of the Family after Joe Pecora died in 1987. Together, Porter and Genovese moved the LaRocca Family headquarters to Genovese's Holiday House, a flashy nightclub and hotel that invested heavily in entertainment. Over the years, the Holiday House had hosted the likes of Tony Bennett and Frank Sinatra, both of whom were known for their relationship to the Italian Mafia. The Holiday House didn't last very long as their HQ, unfortunately, as it burned down in 1988.

In 1986, Tony Grosso was arrested a second time. This was the same Tony Grosso who John LaRocca suspected of ratting out Genovese to the feds, and who both LaRocca and Genovese wanted to have murdered while he was in prison the first time back in 1974. Genovese apparently still had a vendetta against the man; he wasted no time moving into his territory and seizing control of his gambling operation. Grosso lost both his freedom and his businesses, but being in prison likely saved his life.

The rest of the 1980s, by contrast, was fueled by drugs and violence. The LaRoccas took their considerable earnings from their gambling operations and funneled it into building a drug distribution network across Western Pennsylvania and beyond. For a time, the LaRocca Family was the primary source of cocaine for their entire region, being more involved and taking a larger cut of the profits than even most of the Five Families.

For the moment, the drug business was generating unprecedented profit for Genovese and his captains. Only the most successful of bootleggers in the 1920s had such success in Pittsburgh, and the Family used their newfound cash cow to exert their influence even more. In the late '80s, they began making aggressive moves in Erie,

Pennsylvania—traditionally the territory of the Magaddino Family in Buffalo. After a brief conflict, Genovese was successful and took control of the area's gambling and narcotics rackets by the end of the decade. This was the second time that the Pittsburgh Family had challenged Buffalo and emerged victorious. The first was over two decades ago, when LaRocca supported Frank Valenti in breaking Rochester away from Magaddino control. This was a very brief moment of victory for the troubled Family, and it gave off a glimmer of hope that perhaps the Pittsburgh Mafia could continue to be successful where the others were failing. Unfortunately, the conquest of Erie was the last spirited effort of the LaRocca Family before their final death agony.

By this time, the LaRocca Family was obviously no longer observing the old Mafia tradition of only inducting full Sicilians. The underboss Porter was, after all, part Irish. The Family did still tend to abide by the tenet of "Sangue del mio sangue," or "blood of my blood." Genovese and others still believed that having blood relations to other made men would prevent infighting and greed, and would make mobsters more hesitant to become state's witness since it would involve ratting on their own family members.

Unfortunately, it was this exact tradition that brought a crashing end to the short-lived Pittsburgh drug empire. Joe Rosa was the son of LaRocca capo Frank Rosa, and the grandson of another capo, Joe Sica. He was a younger guy, but he had been dealing drugs since before LaRocca died, and had been active in the trade for around four years up to 1987. The year prior, an associate of his named Marvin Droznek sold some cocaine to a couple of undercover cops, and was arrested as a result. Rather than face years in prison, on top of a huge fine, Droznek agreed to co-operate. Since then, he was wearing a hidden recording device every time he spoke to Rosa.

At the same time, Pennsylvania police and the FBI were busy bugging everywhere they could think of to try and catch LaRocca's guys incriminating themselves. Several of Genovese's businesses were invaded with wiretaps, where police overheard discussions related to ongoing criminal investigations. Most damning of these was the discussion of a plan to correct their fraudulent income tax reports before the inevitable indictments for fraud came down. The police found little to directly incriminate Genovese, but they did gather enough from Droznek to bust Joe Rosa for trafficking.

Given that Joe had so much familial connection to the LaRocca Family leadership, one might expect that the tough guy drug baron mafioso would stand up fairly well to the FBI's attempts to turn him against them. But Joe was a young guy, who was now facing the prospect of spending *decades* in prison. Knowing that he might lose his best years to a federal penitentiary, he decided to flip. He began working with the government against his former bosses, namely underboss Charlie Porter and drug lord Louis Raucci. This investigation ultimately doomed the Pittsburgh Mafia.

# CHAPTER 9

## THE DEATH OF THE STEEL CITY MAFIA

Joe Rosa continued to legally co-operate with the feds, and informed on members of the LaRocca Family through the late 1980s. As a result, in April 1990, both Charlie Porter and Louis Raucci were arrested and slapped with several RICO suits, along with several of their close associates. Both of the captains were ultimately convicted, which dealt a crippling blow to the LaRocca Family's drug income. Joe Rosa, for his part, still went to prison, but received an exceedingly lenient sentence of four years. Porter, on the other hand, was facing 28 years behind bars, and Raucci only got off slightly easier with a 27-year stretch (Hodos, 2023).

Even with factors considered for early release, these two were going to be away for a very long time. With Genovese getting older, and much of the top-tier of their leadership either dead or in prison, the Family simply didn't have the strength to maintain all of Porter and Raucci's rackets and keep their narcotics empire intact. Month by month, it crumbled away, and the LaRocca Family began collapsing under its own weight.

Over the first half of the 1990s, Michael Genovese, now in his 70s, began going the way of John LaRocca, handing over more and more of his everyday responsibilities to his most trusted underlings.

Charlie Porter was now out of the picture, so his claim to the throne was null and void. Instead, it was Henry Zottola who inherited most of the job, but he and John Bazzano Jr. formed a kind of committee. Bazzano Jr. was, of course, the son of the late John Bazzano Sr., former boss of the Pittsburgh Mafia. These two comprised the bulk of the muscle in Pittsburgh now. By 1995, they were essentially in control of the Family, with Genovese serving more as a figurehead boss to maintain stability (Hodos, 2023).

But with Porter and Raucci's drug enterprise now defunct, and other gangs quickly moving to fill the void, Genovese, Zottola, and Bazzano Jr. needed new sources of income to keep the Family afloat. In this spirit, they tried in the mid-90s to steer the Family back into their old gambling rackets. As the key move in their aggressive new shift, they made a last-ditch effort to once again break into the casino business, an industry the Family had been largely absent from since the Sans Souci disaster in Cuba in the late 1950s.

The new LaRocca leadership decided to target the Rincon River Oaks Casino as the end goal of their plan. The casino was located in Southern California, near San Diego, on the Rincon Native American Reservation. This was virgin territory for the Pittsburgh mob, whose presence in California generally extended no further than San Jose in the north of the state. It was also a particularly brazen move because they were not the only Mafia Family with their eyes on Rincon. Recently, the Rincon tribe had demolished the attempts of the Chicago Outfit to take a controlling share of the casino. But Zottola was clearly determined. He employed the services of the Columbia Group, a dodgy band of crooked lawyers, lobbyists, and investors, and used them to bribe, coerce, and strong-arm the representatives of the Rincon tribe into bending to their power-sharing agreement over the gambling house. This continued until eventually, Zottola and the other captains were firmly entrenched in the Rincon Reservation.

The success of their financial pressure and the tactics of the Columbia group was a much-needed victory for the ailing Family, but the main problem with the casino still remained: In that part of the country, both slot machines and video poker machines were banned from use in casinos. These two machines were easily the biggest money makers for casinos and all illegal gambling establishments, largely because they were easy to rig and were designed to offer guaranteed payout ratios.

But the LaRocca Family were not necessarily in the business of obeying the law. In April 1995, the Rincon Reservation Casino had its grand opening under new Mafia leadership, and Henry Zottola had several hundred slot and poker machines smuggled in and installed. Perhaps the short-term benefits outweighed the risk in Zottola's eyes, but unfortunately, there were absolutely no benefits to be had. It took exactly one day for police to catch wind of the operation, raid the Rincon River Oaks Casino, and seize every single slot and poker machine in the place, ripping them right out of the floor.

The LaRocca Family's fancy new casino venture now sported nothing but bingo and table card games, whose incomes was paltry in comparison to the slots. The Rincon chugged on for the following few months, but the profits it generated did not even come close to replacing what the Family had lost in the narcotics business. In June 1996, after barely a year of Pittsburgh ownership, the Rincon casino closed its doors and shut down completely. The LaRoccas were handed yet another humiliating disaster, and they were now out millions of dollars that they had in investment capital through the Columbia Group.

Their attempt to re-enter the casino world blew up in spectacular fashion, but their worries were not only financial. In 1997, a total of 17 indictments for fraud, bribery, and illegal transportation of gambling machines were handed down to several made men, as well as to the crooked LaRocca lawyers that helped engineer the scheme (Hodos, 2023). Zottola was among those indicted, and the stress of a potential RICO charge was apparently too much for him. Within a year, the man serving as one half of the LaRocca power structure was dead.

The absolute onslaught of bad luck was not stopping anytime soon. Zottola was dead, several high-ranking members were facing prison time, and John Bazzano Jr. was also advancing in age and becoming incapable of administering the Family on Michael Genovese's behalf. The official boss of the Family was now almost completely isolated. The steadying presence of the Mannarinos was long gone, and his top lieutenants, Charlie Porter and Louis Raucci, were in prison. To make matters worse, Porter, Genovese's former underboss, had been actively co-operating with the government to help take down the Family while behind bars. The information he provided was apparently valuable, as his lawyers successfully argued in court for his release from prison in 2000 due to his contributions, having served less than half of his sentence. Lenny Strollo, another key LaRocca man, was also arrested in 1997, and by 1999, he caved to government pressure and joined the list of his former associates who were now informing on the Pittsburgh Mafia (Hodos, 2023; The American Mafia, n.d.).

The government now had the former Family underboss, Charlie Porter, as a witness, with a slew of his underlings to corroborate his information. Strollo was clearly instrumental as well, as he too received early release in 2012 for his testimonies. Together, Porter and Strollo helped put away dozens of Pittsburgh mobsters, and their peripheral territories were targeted especially aggressively.

By the year 2000, the entire drug trafficking infrastructure that the LaRoccas had built with their gambling fortunes was completely destroyed, and Youngstown—the epicenter of the Naples-Prato-Strollo drug ring—had its entire crew annihilated. Nearly every last member was either dead, in prison, or too old and infirm to take charge. Everywhere across Pittsburgh, New York, and Ohio, the LaRocca Family was losing territory and connections. Before long, they were cloistered in the Steel City, without any powerful friends to speak of and without any kind of financial power.

The Pittsburgh crew may have remained successful for longer than many of the New York City Families, but their downfall was all the more rocky. By 2005, the Family was nothing but a shell of its former self. On October 31, 2006, the old and beleaguered Pittsburgh don Michael Genovese died of cancer at 87 years old. As important a man as Genovese was, his death barely moved the needle in Pittsburgh—the Family was already incapable of making any significant moves. The boss position was taken by John Bazzano Jr., but he lasted just two years in the position before dying in 2008. Next up was Sonny Ciancutti, one of the guys inducted in 1986 by Genovese. He managed to last until July 2021, enduring an endless slew of arrests of his made men and associates. LaRocca guys kept getting murdered or sent to prison, whittling away the Family until finally, Ciancutti became literally the last known made man in the Steel City. The glory days were already long gone, but when Ciancutti died, the Pittsburgh Mafia died along with him.

# CONCLUSION

The fact that the Pittsburgh Mafia is now, by all accounts, completely destroyed, does not diminish the impact they had on American society, nor does the fact that the Family was minor in size when compared to their neighbors in New York. In fact, their small size makes their impact and geographical reach all the more astounding.

Since the days of Prohibition, the Pittsburgh Mafia displayed outsized power and influence. The manufacture and sale of bootlegged liquor propelled what was once a small crew of Sicilians squabbling over local control into the premiere criminal organization in all of Western Pennsylvania and beyond. From liquor to gambling to prostitutes, the Pittsburgh Mafia controlled it all. The good times (and some bad) continued to roll in the Steel City, but the greed and vengeance of these mobsters drenched the streets in blood. To this day, the brutal murder of the Volpe brothers remains the stuff of legends for enthusiasts of both Pittsburgh history and the history of the American Mafia in general.

For Sonny Ciancutti, witnessing the entirety of the Pittsburgh Mafia collapse around him must have been a surreal experience. Sonny's home base had always been New Kensington, which was one of the most important and resourceful of the Family's territories in many ways. He had been in the Mannarino crew since at least the 1960s and worked as a bodyguard for Sam and Kelly, meaning he was at the ground level of one of the most notorious crews in LaRocca Family history. Those glory days were a faded memory by the time it was his turn to run the Family, and slowly he watched as everyone he had ever called boss died around him, until only he remained.

The history of the Pittsburgh Mafia is all the more interesting for the fact that it had a true, definitive ending with Sonny's death. The majority of American Mafia Families, including the Five Families of New York City, carry on even to this day in their hobbled and disorganized manner. Most Families never recovered from the RICO onslaughts of the 1980s, and shows like HBO's *The Sopranos* depict the dejected and deteriorating state of the American Mafia over the following two decades. Now, little is heard of Mafia exploits, other than police busting up an illegal card game here and there. The LaRocca Family, at least, had the dignity of closure, even if it took many years.

# REFERENCES

Capeci, J. (2015). *Mob boss: The life of little Al D'Arco, the man who brought down the mafia.* Thomas Dunne Books.

Cascio, J. (2021, November 8). *This thing of ours is bananas.* Mafia Genealogy

https://mafiagenealogy.com/2021/11/18/this-thing-of-ours-is-bananas/

Cato, J. (2006, November 4). *'Burgh's mob ties sleeps with the fishes.* Trib Total Media.

https://archive.triblive.com/news/burghs-mob-ties-may-sleep-with-the-fishes/

Cipollini, C. (2023, September 12). *The fall of Salvatore Maranzano, and the rise of the new mafia.* The Mob Museum.

https://themobmuseum.org/blog/the-fall-of-salvatore-maranzano-and-the-rise-of-the-new-mafia/

*Conti, Gregorio* (1874-1919) (n.d.). The American Mafia.

https://mob-who.blogspot.com/search/label/Conti

Grann, D. (2000, July 9). *Crimetown USA.* The New Republic.

https://newrepublic.com/article/68973/crimetown-usa

Hodos, P. (2023). *Steel city mafia: Blood, betrayal, and Pittsburgh's last don.* Arcadia Publishing.

*Itkin's Story: A Contradictory Web* (n.d.). Central Intelligence Agency.

https://www.cia.gov/readingroom/docs/CIA-RDP75-00001R000100050003-9.pdf

Jamika, A. (2020, April 29). *Pittsburgh bosses.* The American Mafia.

https://onewal.com/pittsburgh-bosses.html

Lee, J. (2016, October 21). *From Monastero to Genovese, five Pittsburgh mob bosses who made the news.* Penn Live.

https://www.pennlive.com/life/2016/10/pittsburgh_mob_bosses.html

*Man slain in shadow of church* (1919, September 24). The Pittsburgh Press.

https://news.google.com/newspapers?nid=djft3U1LymYC&dat=19190924&printsec=fro ntpage&hl=en

Mellon, S. (n.d.). *The dark years.* Pittsburgh Post-Gazette.

https://newsinteractive.post-gazette.com/prohibition/indexmobile.html

Mullen, L. (2021, April 14). *The murder and mayhem of Pittsburgh's historic mafia.*

West Hills Gazette. https://westhillsgazette.com/the-murder-and-mayhem-of-pittsburghs-historic-mafia/

*Obituary for Salvatore Catanzaro* (1916, February 20). The Pittsburgh Post.

https://www.newspapers.com/article/the-pittsburgh-post-obituary-for-salvato/39731802/?locale=en-CA

Ove, T. (2000, November 6). *Mafia has long history here, growing from bootleg days.* Pittsburgh Post-Gazette.

http://pangallo.freehostia.com/joetheghost.htm

*Pittsburgh (LaRocca) mob leaders* (n.d.). The American Mafia.

https://mafiahistory.us/maf-b-pi.html

Rotenstein, D. (2020, December 22). *Stardust: Pittsburgh's mob outpost in Vegas.* History Sidebar.

https://blog.historian4hire.net/2020/12/22/stardust/

*Today in history: Alcohol prohibition went into effect* (2022, January 17). Kenny,

Burns & McGill. https://www.kennyburnsmcgill.com/blog/today-in-history-alcohol-prohibition-went-into-effect/

U.S. Government (1961, August 23). *Office memorandum.* Archives.gov.

https://www.archives.gov/files/research/jfk/releases/docid-32572440.pdf

Valin, E. (n.d.). *Zeid betrayed Pittsburgh area mobsters.* The American Mafia.

https://mafiahistory.us/rattrap/infzeid.html

www.ingramcontent.com/pod-product-compliance
Lightning Source LLC
Chambersburg PA
CBHW072059110526
44590CB00018B/3244